HOW THE UNITED NATIONS WORKS

HOW THE UNITED

NATIONS WORKS

THIRD EDITION

by Tom Galt

Illustrated by AVA MORGAN

Thomas Y. Crowell Company
NEW YORK

Books by Tom Galt

SEVEN DAYS FROM SUNDAY
THE RISE OF THE THUNDERER
PEACE AND WAR: MAN MADE
PETER ZENGER: FIGHTER FOR FREEDOM
HOW THE UNITED NATIONS WORKS
VOLCANO

SIXTEENTH PRINTING

MANUFACTURED IN THE UNITED STATES OF AMERICA
BY THE VAIL-BALLOU PRESS, BINGHAMTON, NEW YORK

Library of Congress Catalog Card No. 65-13819

FOREWORD

by CARLOS P. ROMULO
*President of the Fourth General Assembly
of the United Nations*

In San Francisco I addressed an appeal to the representatives of the fifty-odd countries who had assembled to organize
the United Nations. I proposed to them that we make the
floor of the United Nations "the last battlefield." I renew this
appeal and I address it not only to governments and the representatives of governments but to all the peoples of the
world. It was they, the peoples of the United Nations, who
wrote into the Charter these four solemn pledges:

"to save succeeding generations from the scourge of
war, which twice in our lifetime has brought untold sorrow to mankind, and

"to reaffirm faith in fundamental human rights, in the
dignity and worth of the human person, in the equal
rights of men and women and of nations large and small,
and

"to establish conditions under which justice and respect for the obligations arising from treaties and other
sources of international law can be maintained, and

"to promote social progress and better standards of life
in larger freedom."

It is they and they alone—the peoples of the world—who

can redeem these pledges and translate them through faithful observance and practice into living reality.

These pledges which they have written into the Charter of the United Nations express mankind's best will for the building of a new kind of world—a free world, a secure world, a world at peace not because there is nothing left worth fighting for but because war has at long last become obsolete.

This job of building a new kind of world is something which the peoples of the United Nations cannot entrust to rulers. It is a job which they cannot delegate to governments. It is something which they will have to do themselves.

"We the peoples of the United Nations . . ." So goes the Charter.

In the final reckoning, the fate of the world will be decided by the peoples of the world. They alone can make the United Nations truly the last battlefield of the age-old fight against war and the first proving ground of a victorious new crusade for permanent peace.

That is why I welcome this book and I congratulate the author for writing it. The peoples of the world must know how this instrument of peace—the only one that we have to-day—works in their interest. Only by an intelligent comprehension of its machinery can they realize the service that it is rendering and the difficulties that confront it constantly. If it is to succeed we must first of all have a working knowledge of its component parts.

Tom Galt deserves the highest praise for undertaking this work in a manner that puts it within the reach even of young readers, whose faith in the United Nations must be strengthened if the United Nations is to grow and develop so that it will succeed in its mission of peace and brotherhood for all mankind.

CONTENTS

vii

Part I—HOW THE UNITED NATIONS BEGAN

"To help
nations to pursue their aspirations
in harmony"
— U Thant

Chapter 1

WHY THE UN WAS FORMED

OUR COUNTRY is a member of the United Nations, which is the most important organization that has ever been created on this earth. You are in it.

Therefore you should know why it was made, what its different parts are, how it works. You need to know what it can do for you and what you can do for it.

The United Nations was created to try to solve a dangerous, growing problem in the world, and to free us from a horrendous danger. These are its two jobs. This story tells why they have to be done:

Mr. Henderson came home one day carrying a great, heavy sledge hammer over his shoulder, scowling and grumbling to himself. He was a big man with red hair and large, powerful hands.

He grumbled all the way up the stairs to his crowded little three-room apartment, where he and his wife and four children had to live.

"It's not fair!" he shouted angrily at his wife. "Six of us have to elbow each other around in these three little rooms, while our neighbor has only his wife and one daughter, and yet they also have three whole rooms! We need to expand, and I'm going to do something about it!"

In one of his rooms he had collected all the things he needed—bricks, cement, a trowel.

Raising his sledge hammer, he swung it violently against the wall. Crash! Down came the plaster! He swung the big hammer again.

In half an hour he had knocked open a hole big enough to walk through into the bedroom of his neighbor's apart-

ment. Bricks and plaster crashed to the floor. He pounded and shaped the hole carefully.

Then he marched across his neighbor's bedroom, opened the door, and looked into the rest of that apartment. No one was at home. The family had gone to spend the afternoon at the zoo.

So Mr. Henderson pulled down that door completely, frame and all, and filled up the space with bricks and cement. Then he set the door up in the hole he had made through the wall of his apartment. Now he had four rooms instead of only three.

When the neighbor and his wife and daughter came home at suppertime, they found their bedroom door blocked up with bricks.

They ran out on the street and shouted to a policeman. "Somebody stole one of our rooms!"

At first he would not believe them, but when he came and saw it himself, he sent for a whole truckful of policemen. They arrested Mr. Henderson and took him to a judge.

Mr. Henderson shook his big fist at the judge and shouted: "It's not fair! My family needs more room! We need to expand!"

The judge answered quietly, "I realize how you feel, and perhaps the government will be able to help your family. Already they are building new apartment houses so there will be better homes for everyone. But stealing is against the laws which have been made by our state legislature.

And we judges and the police have to enforce those laws."

Mr. Henderson scratched his head of red hair. "I don't see why! When Japan wanted to expand, it stole Manchuria from China. When Italy wanted more place in the sun, it grabbed Ethiopia. When Germany wanted more living room, it stole the Sudetenland from Czechoslovakia. And nobody arrested them or did anything to stop them."

"That's true," the judge admitted. "But there was no government of the world ruling over Japan and Italy and Germany. There was no world legislature or congress to make laws, and no world police. That's why nothing was done until those countries began to grab everything and the other nations of the world saw the danger and went to war against them. But here we do have a government with laws and judges and police, so you cannot steal another man's room."

We have made governments for ourselves for two purposes: To build roads and bridges, apartment houses, schools, and anything else we want them to build for us, and to take care of the poorest people, so that life will be more comfortable and pleasant for everyone. And to keep the peace, to try to stop people from robbing, killing, or hurting one another.

The United Nations was created to do those two jobs for the whole world. It lends money to help poor countries build electric power dams and shoe factories. It sends doctors and expert farmers to show townspeople and villagers how to improve their own health and their own farms. The

UN is also trying to prevent soldiers from slaughtering whole cities full of men and women anywhere in the world. If it succeeds, it will free us from the danger of war.

The reason this organization was not made sooner was that it was not possible sooner. It became possible because of new inventions.

If you look under the pictures in your newspaper, sometimes you will see words like "Wirephoto" or "Radiophoto." Those words mean that the photograph was sent by wire or by radio by a machine which can send a picture six thousand miles in about ten minutes.

When your grandfather was a boy he lived in a country where it was hard for people to remember that other countries existed in other parts of the world. Most people looked at their own neighbors every day but very seldom saw even a picture of any person who lived more than a hundred miles away.

Now your television set may show pictures of people fleeing from a volcano or trying to start a war on the other side of the earth while it happens.

Machines have changed what we look at. It is hard for us to forget that Germans and Russians and Chinese and people of other nations all round the world are alive right now.

This is important. It means we shall not blunder along the way our grandparents did, forgetting that other countries exist and not caring what happens to them until a war starts.

A man sitting in an office in New York buys tin in Bolivia. He does not have to go down there. In a radiotelephone conversation he discusses the price and agrees to pay. A man in Arabia buys little steel machine bearings in Sweden. He must have them in a hurry. He merely telegraphs, asking to have them sent in an airplane.

These things—radio, telegraph wires, and business—are making the people of every country depend on the people of other countries.

The one invention that is changing the world most is the airplane.

People fly from one side of the world to the other in less

time than it took a man to go from St. Louis to New Orleans a hundred years ago. Alarm clocks, women's dresses, important machine tools, and many other things that people want are bought in the United States and delivered in South America, Africa, or India a day or two later. Airplanes help nations to live together.

Airplanes are also dangerous. Bombing planes have taught us that no country is safe. When your grandfather was a boy, people said, "Our nation will do as it pleases. Let other nations do as they please, too. Why should we care?" But now we have to care. We cannot do as we please, nor let others do as they please. We have had to join with them to try to make some kind of world order in which bombing planes and the frightful atomic bombs will be controlled, and in which our country can help to control them.

Inventions made a world organization possible and necessary.

Our biggest obstacle is distrust of other peoples. When I was a boy my teachers and my schoolbooks told me, "The United States is always good and noble. We never fought a war except in self-defense. We have always been kind and generous to other countries. But the people of other countries are dishonest and mean. They will always cheat you. They never take baths."

And many people here said, "We can't join any world organization with other nations because we can't trust them. Our country is honest and generous, but foreigners are always trying to cheat us."

A man who had traveled in Mexico told me years ago, "Not all Mexicans are dishonest. Some of them are really very nice." He was not able to think of anything better than that to say about a nation that lives next door to us.

When I was grown up, I studied Spanish and went to live in Mexico for several months. There I saw a monument to the Mexican heroes who had died fighting to defend their homeland against the United States in 1847. I read in Mexican schoolbooks that Mexico is good and noble and never fought a war except in self-defense, that Mexicans have always been kind and generous, even to their enemies, but Uncle Sam is dishonest and selfish, and the United States army invaded Mexico in 1914, chasing a popular Mexican revolutionary hero named Villa.

Once I was talking with an old Mexican man. When he found out that I was from the United States he tried to say something polite. He told me, "It's not true that all people from the United States come down here only to cheat us. Some of them are really very nice." He could not think of anything better than that to say about us.

It seems silly for people in other countries to think most of us are dishonest. It is just as silly for us to think most of them are always cheating.

That is the kind of misunderstanding we have to try to get rid of before the United Nations can keep peace.

Now that your country has taken its place in this great

world organization, you can do your part to make it succeed.

It is possible for you to be a citizen under more than one government at the same time. You live in a city or town, which has a government, and you are a citizen of that city or town. But your city or town is in a state, which also has a government, and you are a citizen of your state, too. The state is in a nation, which has a government; so you are also a citizen of the nation. Your nation has become a member of the United Nations, and you are one of the people of the United Nations.

This organization is the best practical answer that has been tried so far to the big question: By what system can all the countries live together?

President Truman said, after the San Francisco Conference, "It will be just as easy for nations to get along in a Republic of the world as it is for you to get along in the Republic of the United States. Now, when Kansas and Colorado have a quarrel over the water in the Arkansas River, they don't call out the national guard in each state and go to war over it. They bring a suit in the Supreme Court of the United States and abide by the decision. There is not a reason in the world why we cannot do that internationally."

Chapter 2

HOW THE NATIONS CAME TOGETHER

Comrades in Arms and in Peace-Building

WHEN the delegates from the allied nations met in San Francisco on April 25, 1945, to draw a blueprint for an international organization for peace, they began with ideas that had been talked about for a long time.

Plans, many of them surprisingly similar to the Charter of the United Nations which these delegates were about to write, had been written by honest, hopeful thinkers during the last seven centuries. William Penn wrote such a plan.

There was one very simple reason why these plans were not tried: because people did not have modern inventions.

When the British representative on the United Nations Security Council has to vote on an important question, he first calls the Prime Minister in London on the telephone. If they disagree, the representative can get into an airplane and be in London the next day to talk the matter over with the Prime Minister and other important officials. And he can fly back again in a few hours.

Two or three hundred years ago that would have been impossible. If the representatives in a congress of the nations had wanted to consult their own governments then, they would have had to go by stagecoach, on horseback, and in sailboats. By the time they got together again, months would have passed. It was not practical in those days to try to run an organization of the world.

Also, most people in the various nations were not interested in ideas about international organization. They had no telephotos in their newspapers. They had no movie newsreels showing what was going on in other countries. They had no radios or television sets to give them world news. They knew very little about other countries and did not want to have anything to do with them.

When the first Congress of the United States government met in 1789, some of the congressmen coming in wagons and on horseback over muddy roads had to make a journey of more than two weeks to get from their homes in Georgia and New Hampshire to the meeting place in New York City, whereas the representatives coming nowadays to

the General Assembly of the United Nations travel by airplane from the farthest nations of the world in a day or two.

In some ways the whole world now is smaller than the thirteen American colonies were when they got together and formed one government.

Leagues have been tried: for example, a small league in ancient Greece (called the Delphic Amphictyony), the Iroquois Indians' league of the Six Nations, and at last (in 1919) the League of Nations. The idea has been growing through the centuries.

The United Nations came together in fear and hope amid streams of flame, bullets, and bombs. In the days of crisis early in World War II before the United States had entered the fighting, the UN's dramatic story began.

In August 1941 Prime Minister Churchill, head of the British Empire, which was fighting for its very life against the victorious German Nazis, met President Franklin D. Roosevelt of the United States on a battleship "somewhere in the Atlantic." The German armies had just invaded Russia and were advancing so rapidly that it looked as though the Soviet Union might soon be defeated completely, leaving Germany in control of the whole of Europe. England would then be almost entirely alone to fight against the overwhelming power of the Nazis.

At that moment President Roosevelt and Prime Minister Churchill wrote the Atlantic Charter.

It said that the United States sympathized with England. Although we were not yet in the war, we were on England's side.

Most important of all, it said the two countries expected someday "the establishment of a wider and permanent system of general security." The official reports explained that that meant a world organization.

Five months later, on December 7, 1941, Japanese airplanes furiously attacked the United States Navy at Pearl Harbor and sank many of our ships. Germany immediately declared war against the United States.

Within a few days many of the Latin American nations gave their answer to these events. They declared war against Germany and Japan.

A few days later representatives from twenty-six countries, including the United States, met in Washington and signed a Declaration supporting the Atlantic Charter and proudly calling themselves "The United Nations."

The original thirteen states of our country in 1776 had called themselves "The United States of America" some thirteen years before they really became united. And on January 1, 1942, those first twenty-six countries called themselves "The United Nations" long before they were really united. They are not really united yet. Maybe someday they will be.

While they were learning how to work together in fighting against the enemy, more and more people began to ask, "How are we going to keep peace after the war?" Both houses of our Congress voted that they were in favor of making a world organization. Many other people said so, too. The foreign ministers of the United States, Great Britain, China, and the Soviet Union talked over the idea in Moscow in October 1943.

President Roosevelt appointed a committee of men from both houses of Congress and experts from our State Department to write a plan for a world organization. After many months copies were sent to England, China, and the Soviet Union. Those countries had had committees working on the same idea, and within a few days they all sent back plans of their own.

The next step was to put those four plans together to make one. It took two important conferences to do it.

When the Dumbarton Oaks Conference began on August 21, 1944, the Allied armies had freed Paris and the northwest part of France. United States GI's were dying by the thousands in the mountains of Italy and had just

landed in the south of France. Our Russian allies were at
the gates of Warsaw. On all fronts the Germans were fighting in a slow, bloody retreat. In the hot, steaming South
Pacific, American sailors and marines were hopping dan-
gerously from island to island, battling the Japanese.

Dumbarton Oaks is an estate in the outskirts of Washington, D.C. Its peaceful, stately mansion draped with ivy was
built more than a century ago, and the wealthy owners improved it and furnished it expensively and beautifully. In
1940 Harvard University acquired it and opened it to the
public as a museum.

The seventeen-man delegation of the United States,
many in army and navy uniforms, looking solemn and a
little worried, were led up the lawn by Mr. Stettinius, a
young, square-shouldered man in spite of his bushy white
hair. The British leader, the long, thin, heavy-moustached
Sir Alexander Cadogan, seemed more serious than the men
with him. Young Mr. Gromyko, head of the Russian delegation, fooled everyone by looking as though he did not
know anything. The Chinese delegation arrived in western
business suits, ready for business.

The point of the Dumbarton Oaks Conference was that
the governments of the four big nations wanted to find out
whether they could write one plan for a world organization
on which they all could agree.

After the First World War the Covenant of the League
of Nations was written by a committee of men in Paris who
did not take the trouble to find out whether the Senate of

the United States would accept it or not. When it was finished, our Senate rejected it, and the United States never joined the League.

The experience of the League showed that a world organization was not strong enough to keep peace if one of the biggest nations stayed out of it.

In the Dumbarton Oaks Conference the four biggest nations made sure that the new world organization was going to be one that they would all be willing to join.

The plan they wrote, called the Dumbarton Oaks Proposals, was published, and millions of copies were printed so that people could study it.

People did study it.

And thousands wrote letters to those four governments, suggesting ways to improve it.

The diplomats at Dumbarton Oaks ran into some questions which they could not answer. They especially could not agree on how much power each of the big nations ought to have in the Security Council.

But the next February, in the last winter of the war, President Roosevelt, Prime Minister Churchill, and Marshal Stalin of the Soviet Union met at Yalta in the southern part of Russia. (Yalta, a small seaside resort in the Crimea, had only recently been recaptured from the German army.) With the help of their advisers these three men thought up answers which they were all willing to accept and which they hoped the rest of the world would accept. These answers were added to the Dumbarton Oaks Proposals.

At last, after all this work, everything was ready, and the governments of the four large nations invited all the countries that had signed the United Nations Declaration to send delegates to a conference at San Francisco to complete the plan for a world organization which would keep the peace.

When the news was heard that this invitation would go only to the nations at war against Germany or Japan, the countries in South America and the Near East were suddenly stirred to action. The conference was going to be important. Ten more nations declared war on Germany and Japan in time to be able to sign the United Nations Declaration and be invited to San Francisco.

When the delegates began to arrive in April 1945, a dozen nations only recently liberated from the German or Japanese armies were hurriedly organizing their governments. Forty-six nations were represented when the great conference opened. Two months later delegates from fifty nations were on hand to help complete the Charter. Fifty-one signed it.

The day the four hundred delegates met in the San Francisco Opera House, the Russian army encircled Berlin, and the Nazis fought a nightmare battle down in the fifty miles of subway tunnels under the city. Two days later victorious American and Soviet boys met for the first time and shook hands in the middle of Germany, while more of our soldiers fought a slow, costly advance on Okinawa Island close to Japan.

San Francisco itself was not safe. From the red plush seats of the Opera House the delegates of the world's embattled nations looked up at a stage decorated with four huge gold-colored columns symbolizing the four freedoms. Before the blue background between the columns the flags of all the peoples whose hopes were gathered in that room hung silently. In the sky above San Francisco Japanese bombs drifted by on balloons and exploded, luckily, in the hills a few miles away.

The only bright spots at the conference were the turbans of the delegates from India and the white kaffiyeh head-dresses from Saudi Arabia. The quiet crowd was drab with the shadows of war. Four thousand people crowded into the Opera House—official delegates, their many helpers and assistants, and newspapermen. But there was no cheering, no excited speechmaking. These people had come to work, not to make a noise.

Many of the men had risked their lives in battle. Some

had been guerrilla fighters for freedom against foreign invaders. They knew they must get over their disagreements with one another. They read daily reports in the newspapers of the horrible increasing fury of the war. They knew if we ever had a third world war, rocket bombs would be able to destroy every city everywhere. They knew that was what they were gathered at San Francisco to prevent.

They were there to try to write the Charter of a strong international organization which all peace-loving nations would want to join.

The easiest way to write it would have been for two or three men, who considered themselves smarter than anybody else, to go into a room together, lock the door, and do it all by themselves. They could probably have finished it in three or four days.

The hitch would be that they might put in some things that many people would not accept, and they might leave out many good ideas that other people could think of.

The democratic way was to let as many people as possible contribute their ideas.

Before the San Francisco Conference began, the public was so much interested that in the United States alone the State Department was receiving twenty thousand letters a week about it. All these letters were read and sorted, so the officials knew what ideas people wanted to put into the Charter and how many people had written in favor of each idea.

Each of the fifty national delegations arrived in San

Francisco well prepared with papers, notes, ideas, and with assistants, consultants, legal advisers, translators. The United States delegation consisted of 7 official delegates, 29 advisers, 7 members of Congress, 107 assistants, 47 press officers, executive secretaries, librarians, and the officers of forty-two public organizations especially interested in the Charter (wealthy businessmen from the United States Chamber of Commerce, schoolteachers from national educational organizations, serious men who had worked their way up in shops and factories to leadership in labor unions, religious leaders, and many others) plus a large number of self-appointed advisers who had not been invited but were welcomed anyway. All together, more than two thousand people were hard at work on the Charter in San Francisco for two months and one day.

The delegates to the conference divided up into committees. One committee worked for weeks on the preamble of the Charter. Another committee worked on the chapter about the Security Council. Another worked on the chapter about the Trusteeship Council. There was a committee for every part of the Charter.

Every delegate from every nation had a copy of that plan called the Dumbarton Oaks Proposals, which the four big nations had written and which had been printed for people to study in their homes everywhere.

Also, every national delegation brought its own definite ideas for changing the Dumbarton Oaks plan or at least for adding to it. The delegation from Australia, for example, handed in thirty-eight definite ideas which they wanted to put into it. Actually twenty-six of these were put in.

When all the committees had done everything they could to improve their parts of the plan, all the parts were worked together into one document, called the *Charter of the United Nations*.

At last, after two full months of discussing and arguing and settling their differences of opinion, those men and women from every continent in the world met in the Opera House for the last time. Five official copies of the finished Charter lay on a round table on the stage, one in English, one in Chinese, one in Russian, one in French, and one in

Spanish. The chairman called for a vote. Every delegation rose to vote to accept it. None voted against.

The eight delegates from China went up the steps and stood solemnly while their leader delivered a short speech. Then he sat all alone at that large, round table and signed the five copies. One by one they all signed, each man looking very small and a little nervous in such a large place and at such an important moment in the history of the human race. A hundred and forty-nine delegates signed.

The Charter was ready to be printed and sent to the governments of all the United Nations.

A month later the Senate of the United States, by 89 votes for it and only 2 against it, accepted it officially. One by one the governments of the other nations gave it their approval. By October 24, 1945, enough acceptances had been recorded to put it into force as a part of international law, which the nations must obey. October 24 became United Nations Day.

After three more months of preparation, during which all the rest of the fifty-one nations finally accepted the Charter, the organization came to life on a cold, drizzling afternoon, January 10, 1946, when the first General Assembly met in London. Quickly the Security Council, the Secretariat, and the other branches of the United Nations got down to business. The Charter was no longer just a plan. It was the blueprint of a living, working organization.

Part II — FINDING OUR WAY AROUND IN THE UN

Chapter 3

THE GENERAL ASSEMBLY

The Big Town Meeting of the World

WITH THREE raps of his gavel the president calls the General Assembly of the United Nations to order and announces that the meeting has begun. In the large auditorium, with its dramatic slanting wooden walls, the powerful floodlights beam down from the immensely high dome, and a hush comes over the hundreds of men and women at this town meeting of the world.

On the stage, beside the assembly's president, sit the UN secretary general and his assistant. Below them a speaker's desk awaits the first speaker. The main floor of the spacious, airy auditorium is filled by row after row of the big "tables of nations," each member nation having a long table for six people. A thousand spectators sit watching this performance, on which the peace and happiness of the whole world so largely depend.

When the representatives speak, the world is listening. Some of the audience seats and some of the booths with glass windows looking in from high up on the sides of the meeting hall are reserved for newspaper, radio, and television reporters from many countries. The diplomats' words, even their facial expressions and gestures, are carried to millions of eyes and ears round the world. (That is why some governments fear what the men of other nations may say about them there.)

The tables are in alphabetical order, so that photographs show the United Kingdom, the U.S.A. and the U.S.S.R. side by side like friends, though they do not always talk like friends. For this purpose the names posted on the tables are in English, but this does not mean that Afghanistan and Albania may sit in the front row. Each year that privilege is given by the drawing of lots (a ceremony accompanied by champagne and much laughter). Whoever wins gets first place, followed by the others alphabetically. If Norway happens to win, the next seats go to Pakistan, Panama, and so on to Yugoslavia, after which come the delegates from Afghanistan, Albania, and all the rest in order.

Each delegate may speak any one of the five official languages: English, French, Spanish, Russian, or Chinese. These are the languages of the Big Five nations, plus Spanish, added because nineteen member countries speak it. Delegates who speak any of a dozen other languages, of course, face a problem. Each of them must either learn one of the five official languages or bring along an interpreter.

Every delegate is equipped with earphones. Beside his

place he has a dial by which he can tune in the speech in any of the five languages.

When you sit in the audience, you too have earphones and a dial. Once I watched while a Czechoslovak diplomat spoke. As his language, Czech, is not one of the official five, he was free to choose which he would use. He chose

Spanish. Judging by his accent, I guessed he had been Czechoslovak ambassador to some countries in South America and had learned that useful language down there. As he spoke clearly, those of us who knew Spanish could understand him. Others heard his speech in their earphones being translated into English, French, Russian, or Chinese while he talked. How is this done?

In some of the glass-enclosed cubbyholes at the sides of the hall are the interpreters. Each has earphones that bring him the speech as it is being spoken, and a microphone connected with the dial of your earphones. He listens in one language and talks in another. An Englishman may translate from French and from Spanish; an American may work from Russian, French, and Chinese; a Russian from two or three languages. Each talks his own while listening to one of the other four. How many Chinese linguists are needed in their booth depends on how many languages each can understand. A dozen or more interpreters are on duty all the time at each meeting.

Not all the meetings are public like this. The General Assembly, or any of its committees, can hold a private meeting whenever the delegates think it may be useful or necessary. But any decisions made in private have to be announced later in public.

Newspapermen arriving in the morning go to an office maintained for them by the UN Office of Public Information. Chalked on a bulletin board are the most important items of what is happening. And piles of mimeographed press releases have been made ready for them in a number of languages.

Often the assembly sessions are so crowded that observers are allowed to watch on closed-circuit television sets all over the UN buildings and on large television screens in the three big council rooms, where the speeches are piped in—in five languages—on the earphones already there.

The UN has contracts with the major news agencies (the Associated Press, Reuters, Tass, France Presse, and others) and gives pass cards to more than 300 correspondents all year round, to about 2,000 during assembly meetings. They have a club of their own, make their own rules, and discipline one another.

When your paper carries a dateline "United Nations, N.Y.," the story has been dispatched by one of the many reporters granted desk space in the headquarters buildings. During the big meetings the spacious corridors upstairs are crowded with desks and typewriters. Dozens of extra telephone booths are installed during each session.

Every year, beginning on the third Tuesday in September, the General Assembly meets for a few months. It elects its own president and vice-presidents, all from different countries, and chooses various committees. It makes its own rules about what time of day to meet, how long each speaker may talk, what each committee can do, and all other procedures, following the Charter.

As it elects a new president every year and always tries hard to get a good one, a number of very interesting people have rapped that gavel to start a meeting: Madame Pandit of India, Paul Henri Spaak of Belgium, Carlos Romulo of the Philippines, and other very able diplomats.

In case of an emergency a special meeting can be called by the Security Council, or at any one nation's request if a majority of the members are willing. Each keeps a few officials in New York or Washington all the time: an ambassador or at least a consular officer or two. By cable or radio the nations can quickly instruct these men or women to serve in an emergency meeting. This fact makes New York a convenient place for the UN, and a meeting can be called very quickly, even within a few hours.

Each member nation sends five representatives to serve

in the General Assembly, with alternates and assistants to work on the committees. Some delegations consist of a good many people. The one from the United States includes four persons of the rank of ambassador plus dozens of assistants, legal experts, consultants, clerks, and secretaries.

On the other hand, small countries sometimes have difficulty finding enough people for the work. Once when a Central American country was having a revolution, its little staff of UN delegates all flew home, leaving only one girl in New York. For several days she did the best she could to take care of her nation's business, until the trouble was settled and a group of delegates returned.

Each nation pays the salaries of all these people whom it sends.

Each nation decides for itself how it will choose its representatives and alternates. Those from the United States are appointed by our President. He sends their names to the Senate for approval. When the Senate votes against any of them, the President has to find someone else whom the Senate will accept.

One is called the "head of the delegation." He appoints the members of the delegation to serve on the various committees of the General Assembly.

As the UN Charter says only, "Each Member shall have not more than five representatives in the General Assembly" (Article 9), and does not say who they are to be, the assembly has made rules for itself providing that each nation may send any persons whom it considers important enough to represent it.

Emperor Haile Selassie of Ethiopia, Queen Elizabeth of Great Britain, President Nkrumah of Ghana, and President Nasser of Egypt, as well as Nehru of India, Tito of Yugoslavia, Castro of Cuba, and all the Presidents of the U.S.A. since 1945 have at one time or another come in person to speak for their nations.

Although the assembly's business is urgent and its tone generally solemn, the delegates sometimes put in practice what the French playwright Ionesco said: "A person who does not laugh cannot be serious."

Thus when Prime Minister Macmillan of England stepped to the podium in 1960, he remarked, "I am particularly happy to be here under the presidency of the distinguished representative of a country with which mine has had such long and close associations." Sitting ten feet above him, the president of the General Assembly that year was Mr. Boland of Ireland. The whole room burst out laughing.

So also when Premier Khrushchev took off one shoe and pounded it on his nation's table in the assembly room, some people frowned with disapproval, but others were grateful that he gave to the proceedings a gesture that was both unexpected and unusual.

Most of the work of this town meeting of the world is done by its committees. This method saves time. The seven main committees and a number of small ones can meet in different rooms on the same day. This is why each country sends so many delegates and assistant delegates, in order to have at least one person (and maybe a couple more to sit in back of him and help him) at each of several meetings all on Monday at 10 A.M.

Some of these committees are very large, each having a representative from every member nation. Most of the more exciting discussion and speech-making take place at these meetings. To make the work easier, each committee specializes on some subject; one on money questions, another on complaints made by one nation against another, one on plans for improving schools and caring for poor people all over the world. There is a committee for each important part of the United Nations' great job.

The General Assembly usually lets a committee argue out the details and write a recommendation. Then the assembly can discuss it and just vote *yes* or *no*.

This is the way the voting is done. The president of the assembly speaks: "The floor is now open for discussion of the recommendation concerning Portuguese territories in Africa."

The chairman of the Chilean delegation may raise his hand.

"I call upon the Republic of Chile," says the president.

The diplomat makes a motion that this recommendation be put off till next Tuesday afternoon, so that the delegates will have more time to think it over.

Others talk for and against this proposal. As it has been

discussed in committee and in the corridors and in restaurants around town for two weeks, most delegates have already decided whether they think a few more days will make any difference.

"If there are no further observations on this matter," the president announces, "I call for a vote on the motion."

This is a simple question of procedure. Shall they wait till Tuesday or not?

Right away there is a buzz of conversation in many languages. Every nation has only one vote, and the chairman of each delegation is consulting the other representatives at his table as to whether their vote shall be for or against the motion. Then they push one of the voting buttons on their table, green for *yes*, red for *no*, and white for *abstention* (when they prefer not to vote).

Soon the electric recording machine shows the names of eleven nations for the motion, fifty-six against. Eleven and fifty-six make only sixty-seven. About half the nations did not vote. However, the motion for delay has been defeated.

So the president says, "I call for a vote on the committee's recommendation concerning Portuguese territories in Africa."

Again there is a buzz of conversation, as each table of delegates again chooses which button to push. This is not a question of procedure. This time the General Assembly decides whether to urge Portugal to change its administration of Angola, Mozambique, and other territories. The recommendation concerns the lives of 13,000,000 people.

And it has been hotly debated in committee; every vote will please or annoy many persons.

When the General Assembly votes on any simple question of what it will do from day to day, such as whether to meet on Saturdays, the measure is passed if a majority of those who vote are in favor of it. However, for important questions a majority is not enough. If the assembly votes on whether to recommend a plan by which all the nations will cut down the amount of money they are spending for guns and bombs, or any other serious measure, it is not passed unless at least two thirds of the nations voting are for it.

Even so, the most important proposals can be passed with thirty-seven delegations against them. This is fair play. When many nations work together, each one cannot always have its own way. The General Assembly may vote some recommendation that England or Thailand or the United States does not like.

This is democracy, and it is a new idea in international relations. The old League of Nations Assembly could not make any recommendation unless all members were for it. All. Every country had the veto power. Do you think you could run even a baseball team that way?

It does seem odd that thirty-six small countries, each with 3,000,000 people or less (one of them with less than 190,000) have one vote each, while the U.S.A., which has 190,000,000 people, also has only one vote. On the other hand, India is more than twice as big as the U.S.A., China more than three times as big. Should they have more votes?

For secret ballots—for instance, when they elect the assembly president each year—the names of the countries are called one by one. The head of each delegation walks to the front of the room and places a paper ballot in the little box on slender wire legs placed for this purpose to one side of the president's desk. Here two delegates stand, who have been chosen to watch it.

Marching ceremoniously back to his seat, a delegate may put on quite a show. The whole room watched excitedly as Khrushchev in 1960 walked back to his table, clapping Fidel Castro on the shoulder as he went and shaking hands with other friends.

The annual election of president is a dramatic example of how much of the assembly's work is done elsewhere. Each year the delegates bring their ballots to the box to elect a man or woman when no one has been nominated. In the corridors, in restaurants and clubs around town, and in one another's homes these people have discussed it. So eager are they to find someone whom all the divergent religious and political groups will regard as trustworthy and who may make the three-month session run smoothly, that only the most distinguished persons are considered. And nearly every year, although the ballots go into the box when no name has been mentioned openly, somehow one person gets a majority on the very first ballot.

Electing nations to the councils is a great deal harder. Friendships and politics take over. In 1959 the assembly voted fifty-two times during several weeks without giving the necessary two thirds majority to any nation for one of the seats on the Security Council. After a compromise worked out in the corridors, the next ballot did.

No wonder that when nations have been elected to one of the councils, their delegates usually rush up to the assembly president to have their pictures taken, smiling in their moment of triumph.

When dealing with world problems, the General Assembly discusses. And it recommends.

Its delegates discuss any question that might affect the way the nations in the world are treating each other.

That includes practically everything, except what are called the "domestic affairs" of any nation. For example, they could not discuss whether a Democrat or a Republican should be elected governor of your state next year or what should be the speed limits on roads in New Jersey. Local affairs like that are none of their business. But if somebody is selling dope from one country to another or if somebody has a plan for sending teachers from Peru to teach in your school for a year to try to make your classes more interesting, they can discuss those problems and plans because those are international.

Discussion is about the most important activity of the General Assembly. Carried over the radio, in the newspapers, in the movies round the world, the arguments and protests of the representatives in that big, handsome auditorium make a difference in what people think and in the way people vote in elections everywhere.

The General Assembly cannot make laws which the citizens of the whole world would have to obey. It cannot tell you what to do, as the U.S. Congress can. The nations have not yet been willing to give it that much power. But it can recommend. It can recommend, for instance, that every nation should stop people from bringing opium into any country. A copy of this recommendation, printed on very nice paper, is sent to each government. Then some do stop the opium trade, and some do not.

If one nation refuses to do what the General Assembly has recommended—suppose some government lets people sell opium, or suppose one won't accept the plan about exchanging teachers—representatives of the other member nations can then stand up in the General Assembly and make speeches about it. They can try using persuasion.

Actually many problems can be solved this way, and the nations really do many things that the General Assembly recommends.

The General Assembly works on three big jobs: *One,* making life pleasanter and more comfortable for everyone; *two,* keeping peace in the world; *three,* managing the organization.

In the first of these jobs, trying to make life pleasanter and more comfortable, it gets a great deal of assistance from the Economic and Social Council. The chapter on that council will tell more about how it helps the nations to work together:

To help people get better food, clothes, and houses.

To give us all a chance to get jobs.

To help people in each country to buy things more easily from other countries.

To help people in different nations to understand one another by means of paintings, books, movies, radio, and schools and colleges.

To make people healthier, and fight diseases.

To give people more freedom.

The second job, stopping fights between nations, is the business of the Security Council, which we shall talk about

next. But the assembly helps. Whenever two countries are quarreling, or when there is some trouble that might cause two countries to quarrel, that council is supposed to go to work on it immediately. But if the council does not do anything about it, the General Assembly can step in, discuss the trouble, and recommend what it thinks should be done.

Article 12 of the United Nations Charter says the assembly cannot do this when the Security Council is working on the case. That is reasonable. Suppose the General Assembly voted that the Falkland Islands should belong to Argentina, and the Security Council at the same time voted that those islands should belong to England. That would not stop a quarrel. It would start one.

Usually the assembly's part of this job is only to think up general plans for keeping peace, rather than try to settle disputes. The delegates work on plans for getting the nations to change unfriendly immigration laws or selfish ways of importing food or oil or rubber, or unjust treaties that might cause another war.

They discuss how to cut down the amount of money being spent all over the world for guns, tanks, battleships, and other dangerous weapons.

They try to develop international law and discuss how a real system of international law can be made. (We shall say more about international law in the chapter on the International Court of Justice.)

The General Assembly's third job is one that only it can

do. Since it is the branch of the UN in which all member nations are represented, naturally the assembly has to keep the organization going by electing members to the councils and by voting the budget. In this job it can do more than discuss and recommend: it can make final decisions.

It has to vote before any country proposed by the Security Council is allowed to join the United Nations or is expelled.

It elects members for the three councils and, with the Security Council, elects the Court (as we shall explain when we get to them). It makes regulations to guide and protect the Secretariat.

The delegates also discuss how the whole organization might be improved. They have voted amendments to the Charter. A later chapter will tell how amendments can be ratified to change the UN.

The General Assembly controls the money. It has some trouble collecting enough. It is not like a congress or parliament: it cannot levy taxes on people. It can tell the nations how much they ought to pay. But if they do not, it can only scold them and take away their vote.

It decides definitely how much each part of the organization can spend in a year. Thus far the total has been very small, less than one quarter of one per cent of the military budgets of the Big Five nations.

Chapter 4

THE SECURITY COUNCIL

To Keep the Peace

AFTER THE men and women in the General Assembly have talked and argued, and have passed recommendations saying that certain things should be done, they go home or back to other jobs. The small but powerful Security Council is always ready in case trouble breaks out suddenly anywhere in the world.

The Security Council is usually a sort of schoolteacher, who tries to act the way a good schoolteacher should when the children begin to quarrel with each other. It scolds the nations and recommends that they settle their quarrels peacefully.

But when any country attacks another, as North Korea did attack South Korea, it finds out that the Security Council is also the chief of police, able to turn the whole power of the United Nations against a trouble-making country.

"Our powerful neighbor is interfering in the affairs of

my nation," says a diplomat at the long, curved desk, which runs round three quarters of a circle. There is a stir in the green-upholstered armchairs as the other representatives and their advisers sit up to hear what kind of help he wants.

"I have the honor of bringing this matter to the attention of the Security Council, so that the council may investigate the situation and recommend a solution for it."

The president of the council whispers for a moment with the secretary general beside him, while the undersecretary general on the other side of him jots something down on a pad of paper.

Behind the eleven representatives their assistants sit two rows deep. In the center of the circle a dozen officials, and interpreters, are already at work. Every speech is taken down in shorthand and also on a tape recorder.

The president asks, "Does any delegate wish to speak on this subject?"

One representative simply wags a yellow pencil, and a hush creeps over the handsome council chamber, which is specially designed to stop echoes and to preserve a dignified quiet. The blue and gold tapestry on the walls and a thick carpet produce a restful atmosphere in contrast to the excitement of the debate.

While a representative is speaking, his remarks are being translated by interpreters in the glass-windowed booths at the side of the room and can be heard in the earphones at every seat in any of the five languages. And the powerful floodlights in the soundproofed ceiling come on, so that

cameras for movies, for television, and for newspapers can catch every facial expression. Each representative has a separate microphone on the desk in front of him to carry his voice to millions of listeners round the world. Hundreds of newspapermen crowd the gallery, and send their dispatches by telegraph and radio to every country.

Although the room holds about seven hundred people there is no applause after the speeches, no clapping or cheering. The business is too serious for that. Most of the seats are taken by observers from important organizations and from the many nations that are in the UN but are not members of this council. Only a small number of seats are left over for you and me and anyone else who wants to watch.

At the ends of the long, curved desk are extra chairs for the worried, anxious men who come from nations that are not members of the council to plead for protection for their countries against guns and threats. The hopes of housewives and children, the ambitions and cares of fathers, enter the quiet council chamber with them, and these visiting representatives go out again later with sudden new courage or in despair, according to what is decided here.

The Security Council consists of eleven men, one from each of the eleven nations that are members of it.

The five most powerful countries in the world are always members: China, France, the Soviet Union, the United Kingdom, and the United States. (The *United Kingdom* consists of England, Scotland, Wales, and Northern Ireland.)

The other six member nations of the Security Council are elected by the General Assembly. The General Assembly does not elect a man or woman to be a member. It elects a nation.

Three are elected every year for a two-year term, which begins in January. In choosing them the assembly has tried to have all parts of the world represented all the time, by electing nations alternately from western Europe, Asia, and Africa, then from eastern Europe, the Arab countries, and Latin America.

The council has had trouble with its committees. It has a Military Staff Committee, which meets every other week but has sometimes done very little. It has a Disarmament Commission, which has been changed repeatedly, but when will the nations agree to disarm? And the council sets up special committees for special purposes. But it always comes back to the same hard fact: the Security Council has to do its own work.

The council meets whenever any member wants it to. Each delegate, or his assistant, must be within a few miles of headquarters at all times, day and night. In case of an emergency, such as war breaking out in Korea, they can get together very quickly.

More often, however, the cases arrive with diplomatic slowness. For instance, in 1963 Great Britain's delegate sent a letter to the council's president of the month, denouncing attacks by Yemen against Aden. But he did not ask the council to meet. A few days later the Yemeni delegate announced to the newspapers that he would request a council meeting. But he did not. Next day Great Britain's delegate again complained against Yemen by letter. Meanwhile a UN commission visited the troubled area. The secretary general sent a written report to the council delegates. And some of them spoke of it in the General Assembly.

Usually these maneuvers mean that each side hopes the other will be persuaded to change what it is doing, so that a council meeting may not be necessary.

Even when they do go to the council room, they often stand at a little distance from the table discussing one point or another pretty thoroughly before they sit down before the microphones, stenographers, and tape recorders.

The number of meetings, therefore, has ranged all the way from 168 in 1948 down to 5 in 1959, back up to 71 in 1960, and so on.

Most meetings are public. But once in a while the council meets privately, with the secretary general but with no radio, no cameras, no newspapermen. Nobody can find out what is said then, unless the council later consents to let other nations be told.

For discussing whom to elect as secretary general the council usually meets in private.

In July 1956, when Egypt nationalized the Suez Canal, the council met publicly. Then it met privately. Then the delegates from the nations in the dispute gathered in the office of Secretary General Hammarskjöld. Often very important work is done by the council when it is not meeting at all.

Although nearly all the meetings have been in New York, the council can hold special meetings anywhere in the world.

At its beginning the members decided to take the presidency for one month at a time, in alphabetical order. Australia held the presidency at the first meeting, then Brazil; then it was China's turn at the first session in New York. The country whose turn it is can appoint anyone to be its representative, who is then president for a month.

The official representatives at the curved blond wood

desk speak sitting down, but the things they say often make other people's hair stand up. Never before has the world heard diplomats use such blunt, straight-from-the-shoulder talk. Yet, the more heated the argument becomes, the more at ease these men seem to be.

Between meetings they spend a lot of time talking with one another about the disputes the council is working on; so the speeches made in the council room are only a small part of the discussion that takes place.

For instance, the Australian delegate, discussing a question raised by Poland, proposed that the United Nations should investigate Franco Spain. The others did not give any opinion. As soon as the meeting was over, they began talking in twos and threes. It turned out that they all favored the idea of investigating Spain. But if the Australian plan had been voted on in the meeting it would have been

defeated because several delegations objected to the way it was worded. In the course of five days of behind-the-scenes conversations they worked up a new resolution. On the last day three of the men finished it at breakfast over their orange juice, coffee, and bacon and eggs. It was then ready to be discussed openly in a meeting and was passed.

Voting in the Security Council is done by a simple show of hands. An official counts them, and the president announces the result.

When a nation is a member of the Security Council it must decide for itself how its representative will be chosen.

Our representative has the rank of ambassador, and our government pays his salary. He is appointed by the President of the United States, who sends the name to the Senate for approval. If the Senate should vote against him, the President must name someone else. (In other words, he is chosen like our Cabinet officers. And Adlai Stevenson has been three things at once: UN delegate, ambassador, and member of the Cabinet in Washington.)

The men in the Security Council do not vote *Yes* or *No* just because they are feeling cheerful or grumpy that day. Each one votes as his government tells him to.

Our representative must vote according to the opinion that our President has arrived at after talking with men in our State Department and with some of our senators and congressmen. If our representative is in doubt, he calls our secretary of state on the telephone before voting.

And the Charter allows our secretary of state or even our

President to take our representative's place at the Security Council's table. In some of the 1956 meetings on Suez, Mr. Selwyn Lloyd (minister for foreign affairs of Great Britain) and John Foster Dulles (U.S. secretary of state) sat side by side at the table. They voted against each other.

In the Congo crisis the Soviet government supported UN action while a leftist party seemed likely to win there. But when the Congo tide ran the other way the U.S.S.R. withdrew its approval and began to argue that the UN never should have gone in in the first place.

Similarly the United States government, which fought a bitter war from 1860 to 1864 against a secessionist movement at home, was supporting in 1964 a secessionist movement in Kashmir.

When governments vote for their friends, or for their business interests, without enough attention to wisdom or justice, they may be regarded as endangering the UN. On the other hand, we have to accept them as part of the real world, in which people act like people and not like princes in a fairy tale.

The president of the council looks up and down the long, curved desk after the speakers have finished. "If no one else wishes to make any remarks, I will now call for a vote. We have before us a motion to accept the Soviet letter assuring us that their army will soon be out of Iran."

One of the officials counts nine hands raised. This is a simple matter of procedure. If they accept the Soviet promise, they won't discuss the matter again for a while. "The motion is passed," the president announces. Any seven votes are enough to pass a motion about any "procedural" question, that is, a question of what the council will proceed to do next.

But in 1956, when Egypt refused to let Israeli ships through the Suez Canal, Israeli soldiers swarmed across the eastern Egyptian desert and very nearly seized the canal. On October 30 the United States delegate ended a speech to the Security Council by saying, "I therefore move that this council call for an immediate cease-fire and the withdrawal of Israeli forces."

A majority voted for this resolution. France and Great Britain voted against it (because they were sending soldiers into Egypt, too).

The president announced, "The motion is defeated."

A motion like that, which could cause the council to take action, can be passed by seven votes—if the five big nations agree. China, France, the Soviet Union, Great Britain or the United States can *veto* the motion by casting one vote against it.

The veto can be used in several kinds of questions.

It has prevented a nation from joining the UN. (The veto can also prevent a member nation's being suspended or expelled for bad behavior.)

In 1958, when Lebanon and Jordan had requested and received American and British troops to help them put down rebellions that were being fomented by the United Arab Republic, the Security Council voted to enlarge the UN forces in the Middle East to protect those countries. But there was one vote against this measure, the vote of the Soviet Union. Therefore the UN forces were not enlarged.

One of the Big Five can veto any recommendation the council might consider making to settle almost any dispute.

This veto can be used to prevent the council from punishing any country by recommending sanctions against it, ordering a blockade or using military force. In the Security Council the United States or any of the other Big Five nations can always veto the use of military force against itself or against any of its friends.

Why was this veto power written into the UN Charter? The reason is very simple. The Senate of the United States and the Soviet government in the Kremlin made it perfectly clear that neither of them would accept the Charter without it. And the other nations knew they would be silly to try to make a United Nations Organization leaving out the two most powerful countries.

In the UN's first nineteen years 102 vetoes were cast by

the Soviet Union, 4 by France, 3 by Great Britain, 2 by China, none by the U.S.A.

In certain cases the veto cannot be used.

In case of a fight, if an army started burning down villages, the country responsible would not have the power to say, "This is our affair. It is no business of the Security Council to discuss this and try to find out whose fault it is!" The veto cannot be used to stop discussion.

This fact is so important that governments have often worked hard to settle their disputes in order not to have them aired in the council.

There can be no veto when the council votes whether to invite a nonmember nation to send a representative to the long, almost circular, desk. Such a nation must be invited when it is a party to a dispute that the council is going to work on.

In the Cyprus trouble in 1964 Greece, Turkey, and Cyprus (which were not in the council) were invited to send representatives to the meetings and to speak and answer questions, though they of course could not vote.

And whenever the council tries to settle a dispute by peaceful means, any nation in the dispute, even if a member of the council, cannot vote. (In such a case a motion is carried if it receives seven votes, including as many of the Big Five as are not in the dispute.)

The Security Council does not have the same job as the General Assembly. The General Assembly can discuss plans to get rid of disease and make poor people less poor, or to help workers get better wages and better education. The Security Council's job is to keep a war from getting started.

Just that: to keep a war from getting started. Also, it has sometimes had to try to stop one that had begun—as in Israel, in Korea, and in Kashmir.

One difficulty is that any little dispute between any two nations might get worse. Instead of only talking, two nations might get to shouting, and from shouting they might go on to boycotting each other and trying to take each other's business away and firing a few shots across the border, and the first thing you know they are at war.

Consequently the Security Council has to try to see to it that every important dispute between any two nations anywhere gets settled.

When the council hears of a troublesome situation, it investigates. Usually several governments deluge the council with information—more than it needs. But if necessary it can call witnesses. It sometimes sends a team of men to the place of the trouble to ask questions. It has sent observers to Greece and to Kashmir.

Of course, if it finds that the situation is not dangerous, the council can only recommend. It can tell the quarreling nations by what method it thinks they should take care of the trouble.

But in case of real danger the Security Council can put on its police chief's cap and exercise more power than any world organization ever did before. It can, if necessary, ask

all the nations to send battleships, bombing planes, cannon, and men (as it did in Korea) to stop an attacking army.

Because the UN has this power and will use it, the UN must be taken seriously. It has gone much further than the League of Nations ever did.

The UN's power to use the weapons of war is so important that this book will take several chapters to tell how that power works. But first we shall look at the other parts of the organization.

Article 24 of the Charter states that the Security Council's decisions must all obey the principles in Articles 1 and 2, which include the following:

> To see to it that all nations settle their disputes by peaceful means, with justice and with respect for international law.
>
> To let the people of every country have the same rights as the people of any other country.
>
> To let the people of every country decide for themselves who shall govern them and what sort of government they shall have.
>
> Not to interfere in anything that happens inside a nation so long as it does not hurt any other nation.

The General Assembly, where all the nations of the UN are represented, tries to see to it that the Security Council's decisions do fit with those very fine ideals in the Charter.

The assembly, for instance, has several times protested when, in a vote on admission of new members, the Security Council has vetoed the applications of several countries. The assembly voted that the UN is not a gentlemen's exclusive club but is a world organization to which every country ought to be invited.

And if the United States representative voted in a way that seemed wrong, the people of the United States could write letters to their President saying that the vote was wrong. And if enough people wrote such letters the representative might have to change his vote because he has to do what the President says, and the President may have to do what the people say or else be voted out at the next election.

Chapter 5

THE ECONOMIC AND
SOCIAL COUNCIL

To Make Life Better for Us All

T HE ECONOMIC AND SOCIAL COUNCIL is the world's
Department of Sanitation (a polite name for the garbage
collectors) and Department of Streets and Sewers, its
Health Department and Poorhouse and Labor Mediation
Board (which tries to settle strikes and disputes between
employers and workers). If your city government neglected
these problems, many people would soon be very uncom-
fortable in your city and would begin to cause trouble
about them.

The Economic and Social Council is also the Depart-
ment of Parks and Schools and Airports and Employment.
In peacetime it may be the most important part of the
UN.

At the headquarters in New York the eighteen representatives, the secretary general, and an undersecretary general

sit in upholstered armchairs at a long, curved desk, with some fifty advisers behind them and a dozen interpreters and stenographers in front of them. To emphasize that their work is practical, the heating and air-conditioning pipes in the ceiling are uncovered, painted in bold patterns of black, gray, and white. Bare wooden walls stand beside the representatives, dark green round the spectators.

The seven hundred seats in the auditorium are occupied mostly by delegates from organizations doing this same kind of work. Some three hundred and fifty labor unions, business and educational groups are officially consultants to the council, and the leaders sometimes speak at its meetings.

The fights in this council are polite but heated.

A representative may say that freedom of information is the first freedom to work for. He may imply that in some countries the newspapers are not allowed to print the truth. Such strangling of the press would not be tolerated in his country.

Another may answer that we must work for equal rights for all races. He may imply that some countries have laws denying to colored people many rights that white people have. Many states do not allow a colored person to marry anyone he wants to or even walk into the better railroad stations. Laws like that would not be tolerated in his country.

It is hard for nations to work together to solve these problems when people have such strong differences of

opinion. That is exactly why the Economic and Social Council is needed.

For by working together the nations can arrive at many accomplishments that no one nation could achieve alone.

It does not do much good for your country to get rid of a certain kind of disease-carrying mosquito if the people in the next country do nothing about it and their mosquitoes keep flying across the border into your backyard.

Sometimes a small nation is too poor to be able to build

a large dam in a certain river to make electricity, but two nations together could build it and then share the electricity.

Workers organize unions and go through strikes in our country to raise the wages in all the factories that make cotton cloth. Then the factories in some other country five thousand miles away, where workers are paid fifty cents a day, send thousands of tons of cotton cloth to our country and sell it cheaply (since it did not cost much to make). Everybody here buys the foreign cloth because it is cheaper. Our factories that pay good wages have to close down, and our workers lose their jobs.

One country alone cannot solve these problems.

Eighteen nations are members of the Economic and Social Council, and each sends one representative.

Every year the General Assembly elects six nations to this council, each to serve for three years. In choosing them, the assembly tries to keep on it the big nations that can do most for its work, aided by others evenly spread out among the world's principal religions, languages, and political systems.

Each nation that is elected must decide for itself how its representative shall be chosen. In the United States the President appoints him and sends his name to the Senate to vote on. Our Congress pays his salary and makes rules as to what he can do.

Usually the council meets each year in April in New

York, and in July in Geneva. It has also met as far away as Chile. Its own rules provide that a special meeting can be called quickly "on the request of a majority of its members."

Its decisions are by a majority of the members present and voting. These decisions commonly are recommendations to the General Assembly or to the specialized agencies.

It also elects and directs commissions for human rights, against narcotic drugs, on population problems, on world trade, and so on.

The *Commission on Human Rights*, after consulting a great many people and discussing for two and a half years, wrote the *Universal Declaration of Human Rights*. This document says, for instance, that a person has a right to privacy, and no government investigator should ask questions about his personal life. The *Declaration* insists on freedom to think and to say what you think. It describes the basic liberties that make a community civilized.

The Economic and Social Council recommended this

document to the General Assembly. In 1948 in the assembly most of the nations voted for it. It was then published in many languages. Some new national constitutions soon contained parts of it.

The commission prepared conventions (that is, treaties to be signed by many nations) on political rights for women, on freedom of the press and other freedoms. So many nations ratified them that the one on women's rights came into effect in 1954, the one on freedom of the press in 1962.

Besides writing these fine ideals on paper, the commission keeps watch to see how well these rights and freedoms are put into practice in the world. It asks the nations to report what they are doing about these things. And it can receive a petition from any government or any important organization that claims that these rights and freedoms are being denied to some people.

The *Commission on the Status of Women* tries to help

women to get as much pay as men when they do the same job, to be allowed to enter medical and law schools, and to be free from many laws and customs that stop women in various countries from doing some of the things they have a right to do.

Prodded by the UN, more than sixty countries (including France and Mexico but not Switzerland) have recently given women the right to vote.

In November 1959, after long preparation by the Economic and Social Council and its commissions, the General Assembly unanimously adopted the *Declaration of the Rights of the Child,* urging that every child has the right to an adequate preparation for life; that children should be brought up "in a spirit of understanding, tolerance, peace and universal brotherhood"; that mankind owes children the best that it can give.

The *Social Commission* works on prevention of crime and the treatment of lawbreakers after they land in jails. It works for better public housing, old age pensions, workmen's compensation laws. Many nations have invited its experts to help plan government programs of assistance to children who are in jail or whose families are quarreling.

The commission has begun a study of help to grandparents and great-grandparents. It has called meetings of social workers to launch programs for training people to be directors of government work-relief departments and of city settlement houses.

The *Commission on Narcotic Drugs* advises the council on opium, heroin, cocaine, marihuana, and the new synthetic drugs. By a 1946 convention the countries that grow or make the stuff agreed to stop production except for amounts needed in medicine, and the commission collects a great deal of helpful information.

This work has had remarkable results. Where in our grandparents' time dope addicts could buy a shot in almost any drugstore, most police are now instructed to arrest pushers and are using improved methods to catch them. However, a side effect of this change has been the growth of a crime syndicate to sell it illegally.

The biggest job undertaken by the council is the management of its four great *Economic Commissions* for Europe (headquarters in Geneva), for Africa (in Addis

Ababa), for Latin America (in Santiago de Chile), and for Asia and the Far East (in Bangkok).

The one for Africa, for instance, consists of thirty-five nations, plus others as associates. The one for Latin America called a meeting of delegates from all American countries (and some others) to gather in 1964 in Santiago and consider what to do about poverty and starvation, which had been growing worse. Simultaneously the same commission ran a conference in Mexico City of editors from all American countries to plan improvements in newspapers. The commission in Bangkok runs an institute, like a college, giving training courses to government officials from many Asian countries.

In these four economic commissions the nations cooperate in developing electric power, roads, railroads and bridges, more jobs and better education for jobs, and more efficient use of mines, oil wells, and other resources.

The UN International Children's Emergency Fund helps hungry or homeless children after earthquakes, floods, hurricanes or wars, and also in very poor districts. Where children are suffering UNICEF arrives with milk, blankets, medicines.

These UN agencies do not go butting in where they are not invited. Many government officials want to fight children's diseases and are eager to learn how. They write to UNICEF, "Please send us an expert or two if you can."

UNICEF also helps many countries to build factories where milk can be pasteurized for the children or where it

can be dried and powered if most of the people in that country do not have refrigerators. It helps countries to build hospitals and clinics for children and for mothers.

Anybody can give money to this fund. It receives gifts from schools, churches, and any groups that are interested. Of the 23 million dollars that it has been spending each year, 20 per cent comes from these contributions (nearly 2 million dollars a year from the sale of UNICEF greeting cards). The rest is given by governments. Contributions and inquiries should be addressed to UN Children's Fund, United Nations, New York.

Besides the commissions, the Economic and Social Council works with the specialized agencies. The UN Charter gives a particular meaning to the words "specialized agencies."

In addition to the UN, whose main purpose is to prevent war, the nations of the world have set up other big, important organizations for other purposes. The Food and Agriculture Organization, the World Health Organization, the International Labor Organization, for instance, are working to help people get more food, better health, higher wages.

Some of these agencies are very large; practically all the nations in the world belong to them. Each one has a charter of its own, and an assembly like the UN General Assembly. Each employs many clerks, executives, research workers. Each agency collects and spends large sums of money doing its own special kind of work.

Thirteen of them, by agreements with the Economic and Social Council, have become attached to the UN as its "specialized agencies."

They are run by the nations that are members of them. The UN tries to steer them and keep them from wasting time doing each other's work. But it does not control them.

In the summer of 1949 the Economic and Social Council voted that the UN ought to give much more help to poor, under-developed countries. The General Assembly promptly backed up this initiative, created a Technical Assistance Board to guide the work, and called a conference to raise money for it. Many nations gave contributions.

At first the poor countries did not know what to ask for, and two years passed before the aid projects really got under way. But when people discovered what the UN could do, requests came pouring in. In 1958 the UN Special Fund was created (by the General Assembly) to expand this work. Governed by delegates from 24 nations, this fund has accepted voluntary contributions from 106 countries and has given help all round the world.

In those years the whole emphasis of the UN changed. Originally it had been intended merely to stop wars. Now nearly 80 per cent of the money and personnel of the UN and its specialized agencies is being devoted to trying to stop poverty, ignorance, hunger, and frustration.

Many an underdeveloped country is like a young man seeking a good job. Without education he can't get the job. And without wages from the job he can't get the education. So he is trapped. At best he may earn a very poor living at some other job. At worst he may turn to crime and violence. Poor nations do the same. So the UN's aid not only helps them but also reduces the likelihood of war.

The UN never tells a country, "You're doing things wrong. Let us teach you." It never gives assistance that is not wanted.

First a request for aid has to come from the government of the country that needs it. The UN agencies then decide whether to grant the request. This happens often, for in fifteen years some 13,000 specialists have been sent to the developing countries, and about 30,000 persons in those countries have been given special training courses.

The UN will not continue a project unless the receiving country pays its share and gives all necessary cooperation. When a new government is elected in a certain country and announces that it does not like a particular UN project, the project stops immediately.

In any case the UN's help is only temporary. You cannot go on forever teaching a group of farmers how to drain their swamps; after you have taught them, you should go home. The UN will not work at a project unless the local government guarantees that the effects will continue after the UN experts have left.

One third of the money goes to studying what can be done. Often this is enough. In Syria large water supplies were found under the desert; in Pakistan coal and iron ore were found hidden in the hills. When these had been discovered, the people knew what to do.

The UN helps to start mines and factories. Loans of 10 million dollars from the World Bank caused several countries to get 500 million dollars from investors creating industries that had never before been thought possible.

More often the UN experts have to push a little further. In one region the local government said that its own people were "lying around under the trees all day, too lazy to work." A UN team tried an experiment; it gave those people one good meal a day. They quickly became eager to work.

In the Sudan the cattlemen produced leather, most of which was not good enough to export. So they had very little money. Three UN agencies together introduced sturdier bulls, new kinds of feed, and better tanning methods. The local government enforced higher standards. The leather improved and became salable. Obviously this project would never have succeeded unless the cattlemen themselves were persuaded to accept the new methods. Consequently a large part of the UN's work is a combination of educating and persuading.

Nearly half the UN technical assistance money is spent on teaching people modern ways to run a farm, factory, school, or government office.

Usually an expert comes from a country that is not too distant or too different. For instance, a program to teach illiterates how to read and write has to be guided by someone who speaks their language. Two home-economics professors from Argentina were sent to organize college courses in Brazil and Costa Rica. A teachers-college president from Ghana did this work in Tanganyika. Lebanese nurses helped in Libya. A malaria specialist from Ceylon went to Sarawak.

When a country asks for technical assistance, and it is granted, the UN finds the experts and pays their ship or plane fare to that country. But when they arrive, the receiving country pays their local expenses and gives them help. For instance, the experts may need a building to work in (often this is one of the biggest items of expense), and they may want two interpreters and fifty or sixty local schoolteachers or local government officials to explain what is needed and to receive the advice that the experts can give. In providing these aids, the receiving country often spends more money than the UN does.

When this technical assistance program began, most diplomats considered that you were impolite if you mentioned that a third of the people in the world do not have clean water to drink. Someone's feelings might be hurt. But now this fact is no secret, nor is the fact that in large areas most children of school age are not in school, or that these conditions have been growing worse. These problems are discussed in meetings of the Economic and Social Council and of its agencies, where corrective action can be taken.

To carry on its work the council must have lots of information. It can send a committee of trained social workers, lawyers, and other experts to any country to ask questions and see what is going on, although if the government of that country does not want to be investigated, it can refuse to let the committee in, and the council tries to get its information some other way.

Its *Statistical Commission* sends out many questionnaires, which most governments answer, so that an astonishing number of facts are discovered.

Following a General Assembly request for studies on future peaceful uses of the money and manpower now devoted to armies and weapons, the council set up committees for this purpose. The one on housing found, for example, that in many countries one third of the city people live in shanties and shacks constructed of rubbish, that this problem is becoming rapidly worse, and that even very cheap real housing for the world's poor will cost the equivalent of many billions of dollars every year for a long time.

The world's needs for food and education are being similarly studied in the light of what may happen to money and jobs if the big nations begin to spend much less for weapons.

The total finding is that peaceful needs will be far greater than the money and manpower now spent for military purposes.

Chapter 6

THE TRUSTEESHIP COUNCIL

To Free People Who Do Not Rule Themselves

THE TRUSTEESHIP COUNCIL has been the most dramatically successful part of the UN, cheering to Americans who know that our states were once colonies ruled by governors (and soldiers) sent by a distant king who cared very little about us and from whom we won our independence by a desperate struggle.

At the end of the Second World War hundreds of millions of people—about one quarter of the population of the world—lived in colonies where they did not rule themselves.

The UN took charge of some of those places, the ones called "mandated territories." Seized from Germany and Turkey long before, these had been mandated out by the League of Nations. Palestine had been mandated to England, Syria to France. Most of the German possessions in Africa were divided between England and France. New Guinea, in the Pacific Ocean, was mandated to Australia, and several German islands in the Pacific went to Japan. The theory was that these places belonged to the League of Nations, under whose "mandate" (command) these powerful nations ruled them.

Actually this system did not work. When a committee from the League went to see how well its rules were being obeyed on some island mandated to Japan, the Japanese refused to let the committee come ashore. It later turned out that the Japanese had made hiding places for cannon and ammunition on that island, which was exactly what the League had forbidden.

The UN took ten of these colonies, plus one from Italy, under a slightly different system. Once more they were entrusted to France, Great Britain, Australia, New Zealand, Belgium, and the United States. But this time the UN persuaded these ruling powers to let the Trusteeship Council really help.

The council consists, first of all, of the nations that rule places under these agreements. To these are added those of the Big Five that do not have trust territories (the Soviet Union and China). And the General Assembly elects as many others as are needed so that the council will contain as many nations that do not rule trust territories as nations that do. At first the total was twelve members, later only eight.

Each nation that is a member sends one representative (and a good many assistants) and has one vote.

The council makes its own rules for working, and elects its president. All decisions are by majority vote (the Big Five have no veto). It usually meets once a year, beginning late in May.

The council writes a questionnaire asking, "How many schools did you build last year?" and, "Do you allow the people to elect their own city governments?" It asks 247 questions like that. Every nation that governs any trust territory must write a report every year answering this questionnaire.

This council discusses these answers, writes its comments on them, and passes them on to the General Assembly.

The Trusteeship Council does not depend on reports, however. It has the right to send committees to almost all the trusteeship territories to look and ask questions. If any ruling nation were to refuse to let a committee come in, the

council could report that refusal to the General Assembly
or to the Security Council. Consequently they do not
refuse.

One visiting mission used to go out each year. One year
they would cover the trust territories in eastern Africa, next
year western Africa, and the third year the Pacific Ocean
islands. Thus each territory was inspected every three years.
A typical mission consisted of a government official from
the Dominican Republic, one from New Zealand, one
from Thailand, and one from the United States. They took
along interpreters, a few helpers, and some UN guards.
They hired chauffeurs and automobiles or jeeps. (The
General Assembly voted the money for all this.)

People in those territories frequently sent petitions to

the Trusteeship Council, asking for help. In its first five years the council received over seven hundred petitions that it thought worth considering. Even as late as June 1961 some 235 petitions were accepted at a single meeting.

In the council room a small table, with four seats, faces the delegates' horseshoe. Here sit petitioners who have come in person from the territories to make their pleas. Often they are skilled propagandists. "It makes me sad to think of the money my people have spent to send me here. They earn only three or four dollars a year. Yet even the school children have given their pennies. This appeal is so important to them." True or false? The council members ask questions. The UN Secretariat gathers statistics. After years of experience they have learned that some of the most pitiful statements are false, and that some of the most unlikely sounding are true.

Every petitioner claims to represent a large majority of his people. Here came a seven-foot giant from the Marshall Islands. Mr. Olympio came from Togo, Mr. Nyerere from Tanganyika. The council discovered that some of these really did speak for their people, who really did want help.

It helped. In 1960 Mr. Olympio was president of independent Togoland, Mr. Nyerere president of Tanganyika. By 1962 all the former trust territories were governing themselves, except three groups of islands in the Pacific.

Nauru consisted of 4,500 people on a tiny coral peak which had become so bare that they all planned to move away.

New Guinea, under Australian trusteeship, was joined with neighboring Papua. Together, with almost 2,000,000 people, they were being aided toward self-government. In 1963 they began to elect a parliament and delegates to local councils. As they spoke 700 different languages, adult classes in English were established in all the districts.

The Mariana, Caroline, and Marshall islands—2,000 specks in an expanse of ocean the size of the United States but with a total land area about the size of Luxembourg— are governed by the United States. Although the population, some 80,000 people, is divided into several language groups, the Trusteeship Council urged that they be given authority over their own affairs. President Kennedy therefore appointed a Task Force to help them set up three local legislatures, in which they could talk about their own needs. Since we stopped testing atom bombs near Bikini and Eniwetok, the problem has been greatly simplified. And in May 1964 a UN mission returning from those islands made the surprising announcement that it liked what the U.S.A. was doing there. Instead of the blame so often given to colonial powers, the investigators offered praise, especially for the dollars recently spent there on much-needed schools.

The UN Charter also gives the UN authority over all non-self-governing territories, even those outside the trusteeship system. By accepting the Charter the member nations agreed to hand in reports about all their dependencies. They give data such as the amount of taxes collected, how many new roads are built, how many people are punished for crimes, and whether any new schools or hospitals are being built.

The General Assembly took responsibility for this work, appointing the necessary committees.

A worldwide revolution has repeated in modern times the struggle of the American Revolution that began July 4, 1776. With encouragement from the UN the 400,000,000 people of India gained the right to govern themselves; so did the big nations of Indonesia, Pakistan, and Nigeria. One by one several dozen smaller countries recently have risen from colonial status and have become nations.

In many of these efforts the UN helped directly, by negotiating with the ruling power (especially for Indonesia). It even sent soldiers to Israel and the Congo to protect their new independence. And the speeches in the Trusteeship Council and in the General Assembly, the declarations voted there, the findings of their committees, and the warnings by the Security Council greatly helped to direct the force of worldwide public opinion, so that where a few years ago some politicians said it would take a hundred years to free the colonies, now nearly all are free already.

When the last Trust Territory achieves self-government, the Trusteeship Council will vote itself out of existence. U Tin (of Burma), president of the council in 1961, said, "This end is in sight."

The total number of non-self-governing people in the

world was less than the population of France. Because this revolution had gone so far, the General Assembly in December 1960 voted that *all* people should be allowed to govern themselves as soon as possible. (A curious result was the granting of votes to the residents of Washington, D.C.)

Quoting the *Universal Declaration of Human Rights*, the assembly declared that if a colonial people seemed unprepared to exercise the right of self-government because of lack of education, political experience, or economic development, they should be helped with those things at once.

One year later, announcing that military and police action against some colonial peoples had grown worse, the assembly voted another resolution, creating a committee of seventeen nations (later twenty-four) with considerable power to work on this problem.

The committee at once called upon the Secretariat to supply information, began receiving petitions and delegates from colonies (even from Bermuda, whose Negroes want independence), sent experts to investigate on the spot wherever possible, and wrote a new questionnaire to the administering governments. In addition to meetings in New York, the Special Committee of Twenty-Four (as it was soon called) met in various cities in Africa. It later appointed three subcommittees, one on each of the major colonial areas.

Stimulated by this committee, Kenya and Zanzibar, Nyasaland and Northern Rhodesia soon achieved independence. (Zanzibar then joined with Tanganyika.)

Prior to 1961 most ruling nations had reported annually on their distant territories. Spain did not. But, prodded by the new committee, Spain has submitted reports since 1961 on its three small colonies (where less than half a million people live).

Portugal refused to report on Angola, Mozambique, and Guinea, which are inhabited by 13 millions. South Africa refused to report on the former mandated territory of Southwest Africa, inhabited by 500,000.

In July 1963 the Security Council declared that Portugal's administration of its African territories was a threat to peace, and the council recommended an embargo, asking all nations to refrain from sending any weapons or ammunition to Portugal.

Next month the council called upon all nations to stop any sale of weapons to South Africa.

Because the liberation movement had gone so far, the UN could give more and more attention to fewer and fewer colonial people. These were looking over their fences and saying, "Our neighbors got free; why can't we?" And by February 1964 the Special Committee of Twenty-Four had on its hands the threat by more than two dozen African nations to make war (sooner or later) on South Africa and on Portugal to free their colonies. Many delegates in the General Assembly were loudly demanding a final date —within two or three years—for the liberation of *all* colonies.

Chapter 7

THE INTERNATIONAL COURT
OF JUSTICE

Where Nations Are Tried in Court

The laws of your state are made by your state legislature. It consists of men and women elected by the citizens who vote in your state. Each state has its own laws. Some have a law that factories cannot hire children to do work that might make them sick. Some states do not let children work at all. All states have laws against stealing and against throwing stones at windows. In New Jersey the law says a murderer shall be sent to the electric chair; in New Hampshire the law is that he must be hanged.

In other words, your state has laws telling you what you must not do, and it has other laws telling what the state police, the state courts, and the state prisons will do to you if you break one of those laws.

Among nations there are certain agreements called "international laws." They differ from state laws, because we have no international police or prisons to enforce them. A state law is "law" because if you break it you may land in jail, but up to 1945 no person who broke an international law had ever been punished by any international police.

International laws are made in three ways. One way is by treaty. A couple of nations make a treaty in which one says, "We will buy four million tons of coffee each year from you," and the other says, "We will not charge any tariff (or tax) on automobiles that our people buy from you." When the two governments accept that treaty it becomes law for them. (Notice that this is a law for nations, not for individual people.)

Thousands and thousands of treaties have been made. Every nation has many treaties with almost every other nation, and when we speak of international law we usually mean treaties.

But there are also two other kinds, which are less important. Law may be made by custom. When nations have been in the habit of doing things a certain way, that way is recognized as "international law." For example, it is the custom that if one ship robs another far out in the ocean, that is piracy, and pirates can be tried and punished by any nation that catches them, regardless of what nation either the pirates or the robbed ship are from.

That is the custom, and it is also common sense. For the last two centuries people usually have recognized that common-sense ideas about right and wrong should be accepted as international law.

After the American Revolution the governments of England and of the United States together created a small international court to settle disputes left over from that war. Many international courts of one sort or another have been trying cases during the last three hundred years. When the judges have made a decision—and especially when the same sort of decision has been made in a number of cases —we say that that way of deciding a case is the custom. It is then regarded as law.

A third source of international law is books about it, from the great treatise by Hugo Grotius, written over three hundred years ago, to works by Judge G. H. Hackworth of the U.S.A. and other recent scholars. These are accepted as authority for deciding any details that are not mentioned in treaties.

These three kinds of international law are what the International Court of Justice uses in making its decisions.

Article 102 of the Charter states that every member nation must send copies of all its treaties to the Secretariat of the United Nations. The Secretariat prints thousands of copies, so that anyone who wants to can read them. If you live in a large city, you will find these printed copies of treaties in your public library. They look like pamphlets, and they are written in the most uninteresting kind of sentences, but they sometimes say exciting things.

Nations used to make secret treaties. When Richelieu was Prime Minister of France he secretly promised to help Spain against England. Spain, very much pleased, agreed to give him some of the things he wanted. At the same time he secretly promised England that he would help her navy fight against Spain, so England, too, offered him certain things he wanted. Nations were still making secret treaties like that a few years ago.

However, the court naturally cannot let itself get mixed up in such foolishness as secret treaties. So Article 102 says that if any nation makes a secret treaty and does not let the Secretariat print copies for every public library that wants one, the International Court will not accept the treaty and it is not international law.

The League of Nations, which began after World War I, had a Permanent Court of International Justice. Any nations that were quarreling about some treaty or custom could send lawyers to this court, argue their dispute, and let the judges decide. That was a cheaper and safer way than fighting a war.

People spoke of it as the "World Court," and it was the most successful part of the League of Nations. The court tried about sixty cases in twenty-five years. After every case the nations actually did obey the court's decision.

The United States could have subscribed to that World Court and could have taken quarrels to it. But the Senate several times voted not to.

The new International Court of Justice is a part of the United Nations, but it is almost exactly the same as the old World Court. The only changes made were some little details to help the new court work a little more smoothly. The reason our Senate accepted this court in 1945, only ten years after it had for the last time rejected the old World Court, was that the Second World War had caused Americans to take a lot more interest in any world organization or court that might help to keep peace.

Every nation that joins the United Nations has to subscribe to the new International Court of Justice at the same time.

The members of the court, however, are men, not nations. When the General Assembly elects members of the Security Council, the Economic and Social Council, or the Trusteeship Council, it elects nations. Then each elected nation decides for itself how it will choose the man or woman to be its representative. But the judges in this court are not representatives. They do not represent anybody.

The system of nominating and electing them is very complicated, but it works well. The government of each nation appoints four people known as its "national group." This group nominates four judges. All the nominations from all the nations are sent to the Security Council and to the General Assembly. These two bodies vote on them. Any judge who receives a majority vote in the Security Council and also in the General Assembly is elected. (Here there is no veto.)

The result is a court of fifteen men, five elected every third year. No two of them can be from the same nation. They are required to be "independent judges, elected regardless of their nationality from among persons of high

moral character" (Article 2 of the Statute of the Court).
Actually they are very highly respected men.

Each judge serves for nine years and can be re-elected
after that. No judge can be removed until his nine years are
up, and nine years is a long time. When he is deciding a
case he does not ask himself, "Will the General Assembly
dislike this and fire me?" He decides it any way that seems
to him right. If a judge becomes too sick to do his work and
still refuses to resign, the other judges can vote him out, if
they all agree, but no one else can remove him. In other
words, the Security Council and the General Assembly had
better choose judges who can be trusted.

These judges are not allowed to take orders from anybody. If one of them is from the United States, the President of the U.S. is not allowed to tell him how to vote or
even to hint to him how to vote. If a judge does take orders
from anybody, the other judges can vote him out of the
court.

The General Assembly pays the judges' salaries. It cannot reduce a judge's salary during his nine-year term.

The court will not listen to a dispute between individuals. Even if a man who is a citizen of one country claims
that the government of another country has robbed him of
several million dollars, this court will not hear his case,
because he is not a nation. It takes only cases where one
nation has a complaint against another nation.

(However, nations do bring cases that concern one man.

A stormy Peruvian, Haya de la Torre, was the subject of a contention between Peru and Colombia.)

Any member of the UN can bring cases to this court. Also any other nation can ask for that privilege. Switzerland, Liechtenstein, and San Marino, though not members of the UN, have subscribed to the court. They even pay their share of its expenses.

The court does not go out looking for cases. It cannot order any two nations to bring their quarrel to it. The Security Council cannot order any nation to take its complaint to the court, though it can recommend that such action be taken.

The way cases get started is that one nation sends a message to the registrar of the court, saying, "We have a dispute with such and such a nation." This message must also tell what the dispute is about. The registrar immediately notifies the other nation and all the other members of the UN.

If the other nation refuses to come into court on this case, that is the end of that. Nobody can force it to do so. The court can go ahead and try the case while that nation stays away. But such a trial might be a waste of time.

Article 36 of the Statute of the International Court states that any nation can accept what is called the "compulsory jurisdiction" of the court. When a government accepts this, it signs a treaty saying, "If any country shall bring a case against us in the International Court under proper conditions, we now consent in advance to be there, to let the case be tried, and to obey the Court's decision."

Thirty-seven nations, including the United States, have made this promise.

The court does not have to accept every squabble brought to it. Sometimes the court decides, "This is not the kind of case we can try." Quite often it decides, "The nation which is complaining does not have any real complaint; so there is no need for us to trouble ourselves with this."

When a nation says that some other nation has broken a treaty, or has broken some custom which is generally recognized as international law, that case can go to the court. The court's job is to find out whether the accused nation has done what the other claims it has done, and if so, whether it has broken any treaty or other international law.

France and England came to the court with a quarrel over some islands which are very close to the northern shore of France. England claimed to have occupied them for centuries. France claimed that, on the contrary, some of them were not occupied at all but were used by French fishermen for storing their nets in winter.

One piece of evidence was a treaty made in 1360, by which the French king recognized the English king's right to the islands which he "now holds." And in the end the court decided they still belong to England.

Suppose the government of Ecuador claims that Venezuela robbed three citizens of Ecuador of four million dollars' worth of oil wells, which those men had bought in Venezuela. And suppose Venezuela admits that it took the oil wells away from those men.

The court must decide whether this action was contrary to any treaty or to any other sort of international law.

Suppose the court decides that Venezuela had a legal right to take the wells but that it should pay the men for them. Then the court would have to consult experts and

listen to arguments and decide how much money Venezuela owed those men. It might decide that Venezuela owed them one million dollars instead of the four million originally claimed.

Then the government of Venezuela would be obligated to pay one million dollars to the government of Ecuador, which would pay the three men.

Sometimes a nation in a dispute claims, "Yes, that is what the treaty says, but the treaty is unjust and must be changed." That case is not decided by this court. This court's job is to decide whether the nations have obeyed their treaties, not to change a treaty. That case would go either to the Security Council or to the General Assembly.

The court can make its own rules for its meetings, provided it obeys the Statute of the International Court of Justice, which you will find at the back of this book.

It elects one of its own judges to be its president, and chooses someone to be its registrar. The registrar is a sort of chief clerk. With the help of assistants, he keeps records for the court and does any other work they want him to do.

The court usually meets at The Hague in the Netherlands, but it can meet in other places if necessary. It works all year long, except during vacations.

If the court were busy with a lot of cases, it could break up into "chambers" of three or more judges each. There might be four of these chambers hearing four different cases all on the same morning. But this has never occurred.

If one of the judges hearing a case happens to be from

France when the dispute is between France and Poland and there does not happen to be any judge from Poland that year, some people might feel that the court was being unfair. So the Statute provides that in such a situation the government of Poland can appoint a judge from Poland, who will sit with the court on that one case. He will have one vote in the decision just like each of the other judges.

Most cases are heard either in English or in French. If some of the people who come as witnesses or as lawyers do not speak the language that is being used in their case, they have to employ interpreters.

When we say a nation takes a case into court, we mean that the government of that nation appoints a person to be its agent, and he goes into the courtroom with any lawyers, assistants, interpreters, and secretaries whom he may need to help him. He hands the judges any important papers he thinks may prove his side right, and he talks and must answer questions.

The court gets some help (but not so much as the Economic and Social Council gets). If the case is about oil wells, the judges can invite some man who knows about oil wells to sit with them. Such a man is called by the peculiar word "assessor" (Article 30 of the Statute). He may turn to the witnesses or the lawyers and ask them embarrassing questions. He takes part in the discussion which the judges have off in a room by themselves. But he does not vote in the decision.

The court can call other experts simply to stand up in

the courtroom and answer questions. It can call witnesses. It can ask for any papers, letters, treaties, or other evidence it wants.

It has no power for seizing witnesses and evidence. If it wants information about those oil wells in Venezuela, it can only ask the government of Venezuela to send the evidence. It cannot send its own registrar to look and take photographs. If the court wants a witness from France, it can only ask the government of France to send that witness.

This is not really a weakness. Suppose Poland claims, "France made a treaty promising to send us eleven steam turbine engines, and did not send them!" France demands, "Let us send a photographer to Poland to take pictures of the eleven engines, which we did send." Poland refuses to let the French photographer come in.

It is not necessary for the court to send its registrar to look at the engines. The judges simply decide which country they think is lying.

When the two sides have presented their documents and have spoken their speeches, and the judges have finished asking questions, the judges go into a room by themselves and talk it over. Then they vote, and a majority vote decides the case. If the vote is even—say six to six, or five to five—the judge who was president of the court in that case votes twice. His extra vote is called the "casting vote" (Article 55 of the Statute) .

The decision is then written down, together with the

reasons for it. Usually one judge writes the decision, but it gives the names of all the judges who voted for it. One of these decisions, with the reasons carefully stated, usually fills about ten printed pages. Law students read whole books full of them to learn about international law.

Each decision is read aloud in the courtroom, while the agents and lawyers listen, and then copies are printed and sent to anybody who wants them, to governments, libraries, and students.

Then the court's job is done. It makes no effort to force the nations to obey the decision.

Each nation that signs the Charter of the United Nations promises to obey the court's decision on any case between that nation and any other nation. Switzerland, Liechtenstein, and San Marino, too, had to make this promise. Article 94 provides that if one nation does not obey one of these decisions, the other nation in the dispute can send an urgent message about it to the Security Council.

Then the Security Council can go into action. The Charter says sweepingly that in such a case the Security Council can do whatever it thinks necessary. This statement seems rather vague, and in practice, if the disobedient nation is not threatening to start a war, the UN will actually do very little except make recommendations.

The League of Nations did even less; yet all the old World Court's decisions were obeyed. The new International Court has been defied once. It told Albania to pay some money to England, and Albania refused. But in other disputes the nations have been obeying the court, and probably they will continue to obey it.

Why? The reason is very simple. If a nation disregards the court's decisions it will be in trouble. Every other nation from then on can say, "We won't make any more treaties with you because you don't live up to your promises." But a nation cannot exist without making treaties with other nations.

In the years from 1946 to 1962 the court had only thirty-five cases. But in several of these the accused party suddenly became more reasonable and arranged a settlement without waiting for the judges to decide. Many other disputes were worked out in the same way *before* they could be taken to the court. One side merely threatened, "If you don't talk sense, we're going to the World Court!"

On the other hand, when an airplane was shot down over Bulgaria in 1955, Israel, the U.S.A., and Great Britain all brought claims to the court; and Bulgaria simply refused to let the court try the case. So all three claims were useless. Several other incidents of aircraft shot down over various countries ended in stalemate when the accused governments "did not consent" to be sued.

Chapter 8

THE SECRETARIAT

The Men and Women Who Keep the UN Going

WHEN you enter a United Nations office and hear the typewriters clicking and an executive dictating letters, when you attend a meeting and see the stenographers and hear the interpreters, you are seeing the Secretariat. ("Secretariat" is a French word, meaning a group of people who work in a government office.) They supply the day-to-day strength of the organization. They are men and women who devote their energies to making it succeed.

The secretary general, who is the head of the Secretariat, is so important that the nations have always tried very hard to get a good one.

The Security Council looks for a person for this job, and the representatives have to keep hunting till they find someone whom all the Big Five plus at least two smaller members of the Security Council will accept. Then that name goes to the General Assembly. If the General Assembly votes for him, he is elected. If not, the Security Council has to try again till it finds someone whom the General Assembly will vote for.

The secretary general serves for a five-year term and can be re-elected at the end of it. The United Nations pays him a large salary, plus an expense allowance. The first two, Trygve Lie of Norway and Dag Hammarskjöld of Sweden, were followed by U Thant of Burma.

When a nation is slow in appointing a delegate to a committee (occasionally someone forgets), the secretary general telephones to that country's delegation in New York or to its embassy in Washington, telling them to hurry up. He is the UN's chief administrator, to keep the organization going.

He and his assistants prepare the program for each meeting of the Security Council and of the General Assembly. Of course, they can vote to change his program if necessary.

The Charter says he shall attend all the meetings of the General Assembly, the Security Council, the Economic and Social Council, and the Trusteeship Council. Actually two or more of these may meet at the same time. So he sends a deputy, called "undersecretary." But he and his deputies often meet together, because one of their jobs is to let each group know what the others are doing.

They and their assistants attend the meetings of committees, commissions, and subcommissions. These sometimes meet in secret, but they can keep no secrets from the secretary general.

The twelve undersecretaries also manage the Secretariat departments for the General Assembly, for the three councils, and the International Court, also for UN personnel, money and public information, and for four types of UN problems. Mr. Ralph Bunche (of the U.S.A.), for example, has been undersecretary of the department for political affairs, as well as special assistant for civilian aid to the Congo. The undersecretary for the secretariat of the International Court commonly goes to the Hague and opens each case by standing before the fifteen judges and reading to them his preliminary report on the facts and claims.

The most important undersecretary is, of course, the one for the General Assembly. Hence Mr. C. V. Narasimhan (of India), in this post, has been appointed *chef de cabinet*, leader next after U Thant.

These men help direct the meetings, where their information and understanding are often very welcome. But they of course do not vote. The secretary general has the right to speak up in the General Assembly and in all the councils and commissions, even in the Security Council's debates on the use of armed force.

He has one very special job. He might find out that some nation is secretly preparing to attack another, or that some nation is ruling a certain colony so badly that the people are ready to fight about it; or he might hear of any other serious trouble. The secretary general has many ways of finding out such things. Many people send him letters or telegrams or go to him to tell him they have found danger somewhere.

When he thinks he has discovered real trouble, he can call a meeting of the Security Council and tell what he has learned.

Mr. Thant's success in negotiating agreements between nations has increased the prestige of his job, giving the UN even more influence on world affairs than it had before. (In Burmese the word "U" is a title equivalent to "Sir." That is why we speak of U Thant or Mr. Thant but not of Mr. U Thant.)

In August 1963 the governments of Malaya, Indonesia, and the Philippines asked him to find out whether the peoples of North Borneo wished to join the new Federation of Malaysia. He sent a team of investigators to talk with the people and make a survey. When he had heard and read their findings, he reported that the peoples wished to be two separate states, Sabah and Sarawak, in the Federation of Malaysia.

The delegates from the Philippines and Indonesia denounced this report, Indonesia even threatening to fight about it. But they blamed one another and Great Britain, not U Thant. On the contrary, they repeated their expressions of confidence in him, the Indonesian delegate praising "the magnificent way in which he carried out the task."

In October 1962 President Kennedy publicly announced a United States blockade of Cuba by air and by sea to stop the delivery of Russian weapons to Cuba. Quietly, while no one was listening, the United States delegates at the UN informed the Soviet delegates that if Russian missiles were not removed from Cuba at once, American soldiers would enter in force and remove them.

To save the Russians, as far as possible, from the embarrassment of having to back down in public, U Thant stepped into the case. He personally asked the Russians to remove the missiles. Khrushchev replied that for U Thant's sake the missiles would be shipped away. They were.

Every year the secretary general reports to the General Assembly, describing what all the councils, commissions, committees, employees, and specialized agencies have accomplished that year. The General Assembly has a good deal of control over all of them. In this report he can easily make clear what he thinks the General Assembly ought to do about each group. And the representatives take his suggestions seriously because he knows more about what is being done in the organization than most of them do.

The General Assembly makes rules for hiring about four thousand clerks, secretaries, office managers, translators, librarians, printers, and research workers in the Secretariat, and decides how much money is to be spent on their work. Then the secretary general hires and directs them.

He tries to employ men and women from all the member nations. Actually he has hired some from more than ninety-eight countries. But it is more important for him to find good workers than to have every nation included. For they

do not come to work for their homelands. Each works for
the UN, and is not allowed to take orders from the government of his own nation or from any other government, or
from any political party or church.

Although a few Secretariat employees are scattered all
around the world, most of them work in the United
Nations offices in New York. But it is a little as though
they bring a foreign land with them. The New York police
cannot arrest them in performing their official business.

With Secretariat workers from Guatemala, Egypt, India, and all round the earth, most of them men and women of exceptionally great ability, when you come to visit the United Nations you get the feeling that it is really a world organization.

The U.S.A., as host to the UN, has granted it some privileges. But, although all other countries exempt UN salaries from income tax, the U.S.A. taxes the pay checks of American citizens working for the UN. The Secretariat has fought back by sharing the amount of this tax, so that they all help pay it for the minority who are U.S. citizens. Do you think our Congress ought to continue this tiny, irritating gesture, which does much to make all UN people feel unwelcome in our country?

If you walk into the wrong entrance of the headquarters, a blue-uniformed guard makes you feel unwelcome. You may wonder why he does that and why he speaks with a slight foreign accent.

At one of the meetings of the Security Council on the Congo crisis, some innocent-looking spectators suddenly lunged from the gallery to commence a riot. UN guards threw them out. Ever since then the meetings have been protected more carefully.

UN guards are recruited from round the world, selected from a large number of young men who have volunteered. Each must speak several languages, be mentally alert, physically agile, and of unusually reliable character. They are part of the Secretariat.

When a General Assembly session is about to begin, thousands of delegates, assistant delegates, newspapermen, and official observers crowd to the doors, always including some persons pretending to be delegates. The guards have to read each one's credentials (except, of course, those whom they know from long acquaintance). And since the debates inside may concern problems about which many people are ready to kill one another (on remote battlefields or in nearby hallways) the guards have to have authority to question and, if necessary, search everyone.

Visitors who interrupt a meeting to make speeches of their own find themselves escorted out by sturdy UN guards, who, however, expel troublemakers but do not make arrests.

The General Assembly's own rules provide that if any one nation requests an emergency meeting, the Secretariat will telephone or write to all the delegates asking their wish. If a majority consent, the secretary general calls the meeting at once.

When the delegates arrive, the Secretariat helps them by printing a daily *Journal*. Each morning it lists all groups to meet that day, the assembly itself and the councils, commissions, and committees, with the place and time for each. As no one delegate could attend them all the previous day, it gives summaries in English and French of what was done in them then. During full assembly sessions Spanish is added.

Some days as many as eleven meetings occur at once,

each needing translators, stenographers, and guards. One meeting of the Security Council may require fourteen interpreters. They all need the unseen sound and lighting engineers, whose work suddenly becomes conspicuous if one of them goofs. In the council hall you may not notice a desk a little away from the others, for the conference officer. You might notice if he were not there, for it is he who watches out for lights that should be on but are not, for a loud-speaker or earphone system that is too loud or not loud enough, for a delegate who wants a glass of water or a pencil.

On the third floor of the Secretariat building is the office of nongovernmental organizations. Here the teachers' associations, labor unions, church and employer organizations, and other groups send their own delegates. Members of the Secretariat provide them with information and guides, and keep out of their quarrels. Special conferences for over 140 of these private-group delegates meet with the aid of the UN employees in New York and in Geneva every year.

This has to be done because the UN Charter gives special status to these many organizations.

When the General Assembly or the Economic and Social Council or any other branch is about to meet, the lights burn late in many offices of the Secretariat for days or even weeks before, while the specialists get all the documents worded correctly, translated, and mimeographed. Then while the meetings are in session, almost every resolution or plan (some of them fifty pages long) has to be translated, mimeographed, and handed round before the delegates will vote on it. Once the General Assembly had to take a holiday for a day to let the Secretariat get caught up with some particularly long documents.

Now and then the General Assembly or one of the councils votes a recommendation to be sent to all the nations. Who translates it? Who sets it up in type in five languages, prints it, and sends it to the governments? The Secretariat. Usually they print several thousand copies and mail the extra ones to newspapers, libraries, colleges, to the commissions, specialized agencies, and to people who ask for them.

Suddenly somebody jumps up in the General Assembly and says, "But we can't accept this plan! It is contrary to the treaty signed by twenty nations at San Rafael in 1902!" Most of the representatives have never heard of the treaty, and the delegate himself does not have a copy of it. Quite possibly he is mistaken about the year, and it was really 1907. People in the Secretariat rush to a library and hunt for a copy. They translate it, mimeograph five hundred and hand them to the official representatives of all the nations before 11:30 that night, so that they can discuss it intelligently next day.

When the assembly or a council goes home for a rest, they leave a few little orders behind, such as, "A questionnaire shall be written and sent to all the member nations, asking the details of their methods of dealing with juvenile delinquents and their ideas for improving present methods.

The answers are to be sorted, arranged in order, and printed for our next meeting."

A hundred jobs like that, each one enough to keep a group of translators and clerks busy for a month, are likely to be dumped on the Secretariat after any meeting.

It is hard work, but it is interesting. Many of those resolutions and questionnaires bring action that makes a big difference in the homes of millions of families the world over.

The General Assembly decides how much each member nation shall pay (after talking it over to make fairly sure that each is willing to pay the amount asked). And when the General Assembly has decided where this money is to be spent, it is the Secretariat that writes the letters saying, "Please pay now," and makes out the checks. They pay salaries, buy land, build some buildings, pay rent for others in various cities round the world.

As some nations are richer than others, they do not all pay the same, even in proportion to the population. The United States contributes ten cents a year per person. So do Canada, New Zealand, and Sweden. Iceland gives more: twelve cents per person. The UN gets nine cents a head from Australia and England, eight cents from Denmark, seven from Belgium and Luxembourg, six from France and Norway, and so on. But in addition some countries give even larger amounts to the UN for relief and for technical assistance.

When the old League of Nations went out of existence (in 1946) it gave its buildings (the famous Palace of Nations in Geneva), its valuable collection of books, and its records to the UN, for the Secretariat to take care of.

Helped by gifts from John D. Rockefeller, Jr., and from New York City, the UN acquired eighteen acres (six blocks) along the East River. This became an international area because the United States agreed that the UN can actually rule it.

Here the UN built its impressive headquarters. High against the horizon stands the thirty-nine story Secretariat building, a block of steel and glass. Connected with it are the spacious auditoriums for the councils and committees, and the big General Assembly hall.

The Secretariat runs an information bureau to which you can write when you want to learn what some part of the organization is doing (address: Office of Public Information, United Nations, New York). It also publishes a monthly magazine, UN *Monthly Chronicle*, and many books and pamphlets.

In New York you can enter the UN headquarters at Forty-Fifth Street and First Avenue. Many people do, coming from all round the world. In May 1964 the ten millionth visitor (a man from Detroit) was given a special reception. In the vast lobby of the General Assembly the Soviet Union has hung a full-size model of the first sputnik. Downstairs are the bookstore, the post office selling UN stamps, and an international gift shop.

You can get tickets to watch the meetings of the General Assembly or any of the councils, committees, or commissions (except, of course, when they meet in private). The rules for giving out tickets are different for different meetings; so telephone and ask what groups are at work and how you can get in. Since meeting times are often canceled or changed at the last minute, tickets cannot be given long in advance, but teachers can sometimes arrange to bring in whole classes. Tickets are always free.

Guides take visitors to see the main auditorium and a few of the seventeen council rooms near the river. The tall Secretariat building is not shown, but I have often gone there on business. It is a modern office building usually full of people hard at work. Only special visitors (for example, the Queen of Greece) are shown the Hammarskjöld Memorial Library next door, which houses a rapidly expanding collection of reference works. And two floors high in the Secretariat building have been reinforced for the weight of the UN's records and documents.

On the fourth floor below the street are the huge machines of the central air-conditioning. Catering to people from Africa and Iceland, the system allows each office to choose its temperature. With a range of twelve degrees, an Englishman may turn his control dial differently from the way an Indian does. (Usually New Yorkers like it hotter than anyone else.)

On the third floor below the street, in the mail room, thousands of incoming letters are sorted every day. You can speed this job if you address each of yours to a definite division of the UN. By a network of dumbwaiters and conveyor chutes the letters go upstairs, together with books and magazines from the library. (Magazines include such varied items as *Central African Mining Times* and *Bodega Statística del Perú.*)

On the second floor below the street the busy mimeograph and photocopying machines and five printing presses and a bindery consume tons of paper.

On the first floor below the street, next to the visitors' shops and post office, are the projection room showing UN films, the film library, and television production rooms. Under the approaches to the Secretariat building the UN radio studios prepare tape recordings that are flown to broadcasting stations round the world. Here speeches are piped in from all over the UN buildings.

At street level the teletype machines supply news directly to press associations feeding newspapers all over North America. If you have never seen an Arabic typewriter, you have not been in the UN press room. The nearby cable room has a two-way teletyper hooked to Geneva. The New York keyboard types messages in Switzerland. Next to it a roll of paper gradually brings out sentences typed over there.

These buildings were designed by an international team of architects. The halls of the Security Council, Economic and Social Council, and Trusteeship Council were decorated and furnished by Norway, Sweden, and Denmark. Inside and out the headquarters contain fine rugs, paintings, a fountain, and other gifts from many countries.

You are not shown the delegates' lounges. And the delegates serving the member nations do not have offices here. The United States mission to the UN has its own large building across the street, and other countries have their offices round the city. Supplementary headquarters for delegates include even ships, as when in September 1960 the *Baltica* anchored in the East River with Khrushchev and the leaders of several communist countries aboard.

In Geneva you can visit the European headquarters. The UN has had to expand the old League of Nations buildings and add some new ones, for the jobs to be done are often large. In 1964, for instance, the Economic and Social Council played host there to a conference on trade and development; 1,500 delegates came from 120 countries. The Secretariat provided interpreters, stenographers, printers, research experts, and even guides.

And there the ILO, the WHO, the ITU, and the WMO (UN specialized agencies) have their headquarters and employ large numbers of people.

You can write to the secretary general (whose address is United Nations, New York) or to the head of the United States Mission to the UN (address: 799 UN Plaza, N.Y.C. 10017). But especially you should write to the U.S. secretary of state in Washington, as he is responsible for what our delegates do.

The United Nations belongs to you and to me. It is not "they," it is "we." What the various branches decide today or tomorrow is going to affect your schooling, your health, your pocketbook, your happiness. It may protect your very life from a bomb or from starvation caused by war, or it may fail to protect you.

Part III—WHAT THE UN DOES WHEN DANGER THREATENS

Chapter 9

PEACEFUL METHODS

BOLIVIA BUYS wheat from Argentina, and Argentina buys tin from Bolivia. Then Bolivia makes a deal with some other country, which will buy all the Bolivian tin, and there will be none left for Argentina. Argentina gets angry and says, "If you won't sell us tin, we won't sell you any wheat." But Bolivia needs wheat, as almost none is raised there. So Bolivia gets angry and says, "If you won't sell us wheat, we won't sell you rubber." But Argentina needs rubber; so Argentina becomes more angry and says, "Then we won't sell you any beef!" But Bolivia needs beef. And so it might go on.

If either of these nations is breaking a treaty, the other can take the case to the International Court of Justice.

Or if they think the tangle they have got themselves into might be unraveled by study and the help of other nations, one of them might take the case to the Economic and Social Council. Sometimes the Economic and Social

Council discovers that actually seven or eight nations are mixed up in this difficulty and that what they need is a plan. So the council, after private talks with diplomats from those countries, calls a conference at which they all meet in the presence of representatives from some of their largest customers, to discuss a plan written by the council's experts. Always such a plan gets changed in the conference. And then, if they all accept it, they can begin buying wheat and tin and rubber and beef from each other again.

But suppose one of these nations has tried every peaceful method it can think of, and these methods have not worked, or they are working too slowly and the nation cannot wait. It sends a long telegram to the powerful Security Council. Or it can even send an official with flashing dark eyes and a briefcase full of papers, with any number of consultants, assistants, secretaries, experts, and interpreters to help him, to speak to the Security Council.

The Security Council will listen and ask questions. Article 35 gives every nation, no matter whether it is one of the United Nations or not, the right to bring its disputes to the attention of the Security Council. (When a nation that has not signed the Charter wants to get the ear of the Security Council, that nation has to make a special promise that it will settle its quarrel by peaceful means.)

Any nation that is a member of the United Nations can bring any case to the Security Council. They often do this simply because they see that it needs to be done, even though they are not concerned in the dispute in any way.

In 1947, when war threatened between the Netherlands and Indonesia (a former Dutch colony), the case was brought to the Security Council by Australia, which was a near neighbor and happened to be on the council that year. In April 1964 fifty-eight nations together sent a message to the Security Council asking it to consider "the serious situation existing in South Africa," especially the *apartheid* racial policy, which they said was "disturbing to international peace."

When the council learns of possible danger somewhere, it can appoint a committee of people who know about that particular kind of trouble and send them to investigate. The General Assembly also sent observers, for instance, to the borders of Greece in 1952.

A few years later, in 1958, the assembly sent three civilian observers, aided by two hundred military observers, to Lebanon, which had complained that it was being attacked by its Arab neighbors. Just four months later this team's work had been so successful that an agreement signed by ten Arab nations, ending the crisis, was accepted unanimously by the General Assembly.

The Security Council does not have to wait till two nations are actually pointing guns at each other. It can go to work as soon as it hears of any situation that might cause nations to fight.

Suppose the people in some Moslem country are getting angry because a lot of Christian businessmen and engineers are coming in and building derricks for oil wells. The Moslem government has done nothing about it. The people march in big parades protesting against the foreigners who take their country's oil. The people go to big political meetings, where the orators shout, "If any more Christians come to our country, we will shoot them!" The government still does nothing.

That is what is called a "situation."

It is not a quarrel between two nations. Not yet. But in about two more days it is likely to become one. What will happen if a couple of those foreign engineers are killed? Their nation will cry at the government of the Moslem nation, "Why didn't you do something to prevent this shooting? You knew it was going to happen, and you sat by and did nothing! We demand justice! You pay us two million dollars, or we'll send an army and take half your land away from you to make up for this outrage!"

You see why a "situation" can be dangerous.

The council can choose a method for taking care of the trouble and can send a message suggesting that the governments should use that method right away.

When a "situation" has developed into a quarrel, the council may still have to send that same message. Although the nations have promised "to seek a solution by . . . peaceful means of their own choice" (Article 33), sometimes they do not want to. Sometimes the politicians in a certain government think, "Let's not settle this quarrel with our neighbor, because we won't gain very much by settling it now. Let's wait till it gets worse. In fact, maybe we can help to make it worse. And when it gets really bad maybe our people will become so angry at our neighbor that we can lead our people to war and conquer our neighbor's whole country!" Politicians have often thought that. Article 33 says the Security Council can "call upon the parties to settle their dispute." It can tell them, "You have a quarrel on your hands! Wake up! Do something about it!"

The Security Council can even call upon two nations that are not members of the United Nations to settle their quarrel. This is a world organization, and Article 2, paragraph 6, gives the Security Council just as much power over nations that do not join as over nations that do.

The Security Council walks up to the two quarreling nations carrying a lily of peace in one hand and holding a huge club behind its back with the other. "We're all friends, aren't we?" it asks sweetly. "You will settle this in some friendly way, OR ELSE . . . !"

In 1947 the British government turned over its trust territory of Palestine to the UN. The General Assembly sent a committee to get the facts, then recommended dividing the country into two nations, Arab and Jewish. The Jews called their new nation Israel and accepted the boundary line that had been suggested by the UN General Assembly. The neighboring Arab states on all sides attacked, and the Israelis fought back in a brisk and desperate war.

A UN Commission, led by Count Folke Bernadotte, began negotiations to stop the fighting. Bernadotte was murdered on the job. But basically human beings are not stopped by danger; the same boldness that makes wars possible makes peace work possible, too. The UN sent Dr. Ralph Bunche with seven hundred military observers and representatives from thirty-seven nations. The Security Council backed him up with a warning to the Arab states that if they did not accept its recommended cease-fire, the council would use force to make them do so. By early 1949 he persuaded both sides to accept a truce, which halted the fighting. (For his skill in this difficult task Dr. Bunche was later awarded a Nobel Peace Prize.)

Similarly in January 1949 the council, because of fighting in Indonesia, recommended that that colony should become a self-governing nation. As the Netherlands had ruled it and was unwilling to give it up without a struggle, the council appointed a UN commission to go to Amsterdam and to Jakarta and oversee the long, hard task of putting that "recommendation" into effect. Ten months later the UN commission got the two sides to sign the documents of transfer of sovereignty. But another year passed before the commission reported that its work was done.

Article 33 gives a long list of friendly methods by which two nations can settle their own quarrel.

By "negotiation"—that is, talking it over.

By "enquiry"—they may want to consult witnesses to find out what really is happening.

By "mediation"—two quarreling nations agree to let some outsiders help them find a way to agree. These outsiders may be sent by the UN, as were Count Bernadotte and Dr. Bunche in Palestine.

By "conciliation"—each nation offers to give up something to the other in order to become friends again.

By "arbitration." Paraguay and Bolivia, after fighting the Chaco War for three years, finally agreed to let six men *arbitrate* between them. The six men were presidents of American republics, one of them Franklin D. Roosevelt. These six men studied the dispute and settled it. They awarded most of the Chaco land to Paraguay but gave Bolivia a way of getting to a certain river, which was what Bolivia really wanted. This award was accepted by both nations in 1935 and there was no more fighting.

By "judicial settlement"—that is, by taking the case to the International Court of Justice—or to one of the smaller international courts (for example, the United States and Canada have a special court that often settles disputes between them).

By "regional arrangements." The Organization of American States has arranged that in case any country in North or South America threatens or attacks another, all the rest immediately consult one another. They send telegrams and telephone messages to each other about it, and sometimes call their ambassadors in Washington to a meeting to talk it over. What they do in each crisis depends on what they can agree on.

More often one of the quarreling nations comes to the council to complain. In 1946 a delegate from Iran (which was not on the council) presented the UN's first case, asserting that Russian soldiers were aiding a separatist political movement in northern Iran. The council first called on the two countries to negotiate their dispute, then requested them to report on progress made in withdrawal of the soldiers. Despite harsh words by both sides, the mere fact of having the case aired so publicly did cause them to resume negotiations, and the soldiers were withdrawn.

In January 1964 the Security Council met to hear a complaint by Panama against the U.S.A. about riots in the Canal Zone. However, a telegram from the Organization of American States was read, stating that the OAS had taken up the case that morning. The council therefore recommended only that the two nations should try to avoid any further violence.

The OAS, which is a kind of UN of the Western Hemisphere, has a General Assembly of its own, consisting usually of the U.S. secretary of state and all the Latin American ambassadors in Washington. Emergency meetings can be called quickly, and its Peace Committee of five diplomats can move even faster. Or, when the OAS assembly wishes to gather elsewhere, as it often does (in Rio de Janeiro, for example), each nation sends any high official whom it considers sufficiently important.

It has a permanent secretariat in Washington, called the Pan American Union.

In the Canal Zone dispute the OAS brusquely threatened both sides with serious consequences if they did not stop shouting and begin negotiating. Fortunately the organization has a good deal of prestige; both sides listened;

the shouting did stop; and negotiations began. The UN Charter (Article 52) gives the OAS the right to handle these crises without interference from the Security Council.

When the council thinks it cannot help by saying, "Go settle your quarrel," it can say, "Come here, and we will settle your quarrel for you." When it decides to do that, it can study all the facts, call witnesses, listen to arguments, and recommend an actual solution. It can recommend that nation A should pay a million dollars to nation B, or that a certain nation should cut its tariff on tin cans to one half what it has been charging, and so on. It can never force any nation to do any of these things, but it can recommend.

Once in a while the reason why other methods have not settled a quarrel is that it is caused by some old treaty. A case like that usually goes to the General Assembly.

For example, once a man made himself dictator of a South American country and forced everyone to do whatever he wanted. He made a treaty with a foreign government, which promised to buy all the oil from his country. And he sold the oil at a low price because on the side, secretly, he made a deal that they would give him personally a bribe of one cent on every gallon. This bribe was not mentioned in the treaty, but it was paid every year. Soon he became one of the richest men in the world.

After many years the people of his country drove the dictator out and elected a democratic government. The new president discovered to his horror that his country had a treaty to sell all its oil at a ridiculously low price. What could he do? A treaty is a treaty. It is international law. You have to obey it. But what if it is a bad treaty?

Now that country can complain to the General Assembly. If the General Assembly votes to recommend that in the name of justice a treaty should be changed, the little country can then send a message to the big country asking it to consent to change the treaty, and the big country is morally obliged to do so.

But sometimes a country says, "This treaty must be changed, or we will fight!" Preventing fights is the Security Council's job. In that case the Security Council studies the quarrel and can recommend that the treaty be changed.

Back in 1930, when there was a democratic government in Germany, many Germans said that the Versailles Treaty was strangling their nation and that the treaty should be changed. Some people in England and in the United States thought so, too. But nothing was done about it, and the German people became so angry that, when Hitler promised he would change the Versailles Treaty, they let him and his Nazis take control of Germany and prepare them for war.

If the Security Council had existed then, with the United States as a member, and if it had voted to recommend that the treaty be changed, perhaps there never would have been a Second World War.

Chapter 10

FIRST STEPS TOWARD USING FORCE

Mussolini, the dictator of Italy, decided to grab Ethiopia. He got the Italian army ready and caused his newspapers to make violent attacks (in words) against Ethiopia.

Then there was a real battle, in December 1934, between Ethiopian and Italian soldiers on the border between Ethiopia and the Italian colony Somaliland. The League of Nations appointed a group of judges to decide whose fault that was, but the judges never did decide. Mussolini shouted that the Ethiopians had attacked the Italians.

With this excuse he sent a great many ships full of soldiers, tanks, cannons, bombs, airplanes, and poison gas. As these ships passed through the Suez Canal, which was controlled by England, the English authorities found out what was in them, and newspapers told the whole world about it. Those Italian forces invaded Ethiopia.

Then at last the League of Nations did something. But

it was too late. Mussolini's soldiers went ahead and conquered the whole country.

The League of Nations had no authority to act until a
war had begun.

* Now when a military campaign is being prepared, the
Security Council does not have to wait. If the Security
Council had existed in those days, it would have gone to
work when Mussolini ordered his army to get ready and his
newspapers to print insults against Ethiopia. The council
might have decided that that was a "threat to the peace."
(It was.)

Mussolini claimed that Ethiopia was threatening him.
We know that that was silly. But in every dispute each side

always claims that the other is at fault. The Security Council decides which really is, or if they both are.

The council can act immediately. At the first threat to the peace it puts on its police chief's cap, throws the lily of peace into a corner, lays its big club on the table right in plain sight, and begins spitting on its hands.

There are also two other actions that can make it throw away that lily of peace.

In December 1934, when that battle took place on the border between Ethiopia and Italian Somaliland, if the Security Council had existed, it would have had to decide whether that was a "breach of the peace." (It was.)

Finally, when the Italian army began going through the Suez Canal on its way toward Ethiopia, the Security Council would have had to decide whether that was an "act of aggression." (It was.)

The dictionary says that "aggression" means beginning a quarrel, and that it can be done in two different ways. If you shake your fist at someone and call him a dirty louse, and if you keep on doing this when he has done nothing to you, you are being aggressive. (Nations do this so often, the council has a hard time deciding when they are serious.) Or if you hit him when he has done nothing to you, you are being aggressive. If the council votes that a nation has begun a quarrel either of these ways, the UN can send soldiers, airplanes, and battleships to stop it.

In any dangerous situation the Security Council does not have to wait. If a dispute is being tried before the International Court or is being studied by the Economic and Social Council or by the General Assembly, and that dispute begins to look as though it might cause a war, the Security Council can go to work on it immediately without waiting for whatever the others may do.

One kind of war is sometimes outside the Security Council's power. When two groups of people in the same country fight each other, that is called a civil war. If a civil war does not threaten to cause a war between nations, the council cannot interfere. Some civil wars do spread out and become international wars, and some do not. When a civil war is being fought, the council must discuss it and decide.

The veto power of the Big Five can be used in some of these cases and not in others.

In February 1946 delegates from Syria and Lebanon asked the Security Council to expel the British and French soldiers from those countries. The troops, which had gone there to free those countries during the Second World War, were no longer welcome in peacetime. After some discussion the delegates admitted that they saw no threat to the peace nor breach of the peace. Therefore, when the council voted to ask Great Britain and France to take the soldiers away, those two big nations could not use any veto. (And they did take their soldiers away.)

On the other hand, in 1956, when the Hungarian government invited Russian soldiers in to help put down a popular rebellion, battles were fought in the streets. And when the council voted by a large majority to recommend that the Soviet Union remove its troops, the Soviet delegate vetoed that recommendation. In case of real fighting the Big Five nations can veto any UN move against themselves.

These moves, when they are made, are of two sorts. In case of a threat to the peace or a breach of the peace the council (if not stopped by a veto) can recommend a remedy or it can take action. Often it does both at once.

First, it can sometimes do a lot of good by recommending temporary measures right away.

In the case of a battle near a border it can say to both sides, "We recommend that you each take your army three miles back from the border, while we discuss what will be the best way to settle this trouble."

If one nation has seized some citizens of another nation and is going to shoot them, and the other nation threatens to fight about it, the council can say, "We recommend that you do not shoot those people. Just hold onto them quietly until we have time to look into this matter."

Of course, if any nation is attacked with guns and bombs, it has a perfect right to fight just as hard as it can to defend itself while the Security Council is deciding what to do. In fact, it has a right to keep on fighting and get other nations to help, until the Security Council has succeeded in stopping the attack and getting all the attackers away.

However, the nations have this right of self-defense only

if one of them is attacked by cannons, tanks, or bombs. An attack by words or by money or by business methods does not give any nation this right.

When the Security Council decides to act, that does not mean it will necessarily start killing people. It can try other powerful methods.

First, it can call upon all the member nations to break off diplomatic relations with the offending country.

This is not what we call "using peaceful means." When the Security Council votes for these steps it votes to punish a whole nation of men, women, and children.

When we break off diplomatic relations with a country we order our ambassador to come home. We send away their ambassador. They lose the privilege of asking us to make a treaty of any kind with them. It becomes difficult for them to complain to us if we break some old treaty with them. It becomes difficult for them to ask us to lend them money, or to ask us to pay for things we have bought from them. If one nation finds itself cut off that way from all other nations, it will suffer.

If that is not enough, the Security Council can vote to impose "sanctions."

If you start fights, the teacher may make you stay in after school, or not let you act in the next play your class gives. Or your mother may tell you you can't go to the movies; or your father may stop your allowance. They are using "sanctions" against you. A sanction is taking some privilege away from you because you have misbehaved.

(Or they may spank you. That would be using force against you. We'll talk about that subject in the next chapter.)

When the Security Council votes to impose sanctions to try to make a nation stop causing trouble, the council calls upon all the member nations to forbid anyone to buy things from that nation or sell things to it. Sometimes the Security Council may try to stop just a few things— perhaps guns, gasoline, coal, and rubber tires; or it can clamp down on absolutely everything. If necessary it can also call upon all the member nations to forbid anyone to lend money or pay debts to anybody in that nation.

The Security Council can call upon the countries near that nation to stop all railroad trains, busses, automobiles, or trucks from going into it. The council can call upon all member nations to stop all ships or airplanes from going to it, and to stop all telegrams, radio messages, or letters from going to it.

In 1935 the League of Nations voted to use sanctions against Italy, because Italy had invaded Ethiopia. However, the vote was taken in the League Assembly of fifty-one nations, and sanctions could be imposed only by unanimous vote. Nothing could be included except what they would *all* agree on. The League called upon its member nations to forbid anyone to sell guns or arms of any kind to Italy, or raw materials such as coal and lumber, or to lend Italy any money. But the most important item, gasoline for tanks and airplanes, was not included, because some of the fifty-one nations would not agree to include it.

So Italy received gasoline and went right ahead and conquered Ethiopia.

The United Nations is not like the old League. Sanctions are voted by the Security Council, in which only eleven nations are members, and only seven of them (including all the Big Five) need to agree on what items are to be included in the sanctions.

However, that means that none of these measures can be taken against one of the Big Five, which can veto them.

In 1962 and 1963 two nations were blacklisted: the Republic of South Africa and Portugal. All other nations were requested not to give or sell them any weapons.

And if sanctions do not stop the offending states, there is plenty more the Security Council or the General Assembly can do.

Chapter 11

IF FORCE IS NEEDED

ACCORDING to the Charter the UN was to have had soldiers, machine guns, troop-carrying vehicles, and planes. These were to be used only to stop wars. And they were to be controlled by the Security Council.

This idea has never been carried out. But in order to understand the method used now, we must look briefly at the original plan (which is still in the UN Charter).

Each nation was to keep a part of this UN force. The Security Council was to sign a treaty with each member of the United Nations, deciding how many soldiers, what kind of weapons, and how much military equipment that nation would hold in readiness for the UN. (They never have written any of these treaties.)

The Security Council, with the assistance of the *Military Staff Committee*, was to map out what these UN forces would do in any emergency. And in action the Military Staff Committee should direct them. We will describe this committee in detail, because it is the only part of this plan that does exist.

Each nation has a group of the highest officers in its military forces, called its General Staff, whose job is to do the mental work for any fighting. And these officers are headed by their Chief of Staff. Each Chief of Staff in the Big Five (the United States, the Soviet Union, Great Britain, France, and China) does send three men to UN headquarters in New York, representing his army, navy, and air force. The fifteen men together are the Military Staff Committee.

It is a branch of the Security Council. It meets every two weeks. But you rarely hear of it, as it is extremely tight-lipped; and you can never watch it, because it always meets in private.

But because of disagreement among the Big Five nations UN action has in fact been taken differently. A typical example is the force sent to Cyprus in 1964. Secretary General U Thant called for volunteers. Six nations voluntarily sent soldiers and weapons; twenty nations contributed money. These were put in the charge of General Gyani (of India), an employee of the Secretariat.

This force did not attempt to conquer anything, for the Security Council had instructed it merely "to prevent a recurrence of fighting" in Cyprus.

That, also, is typical. For in any troublesome situation the UN Charter lists a series of steps that any UN force can take, rather than start a fight themselves.

They can try making "demonstrations." They can run battleships near shore in broad daylight near the cities where plenty of people can see them. The planes can fly over at night and drop bright flares, which everyone will see. That will make the people think, "What will happen if they drop bombs tomorrow night?" How would you feel if you saw those battleships, and those bright lights floating down over your house? The airplanes can scatter hundreds of thousands of printed leaflets warning the people what will happen to them if their government does not stop causing trouble.

"Demonstrating" is what the UN army did in the last battle in the Congo January 31, 1963. They brought up soldiers and guns enough to convince the rebels, who then yielded without shooting. So the battle was staged but not fought.

Or, the UN can set up a blockade. If the member nations cooperate, it can order their submarines, airplanes, and battleships to seize all ships coming from that country, and to prevent any ship or airplane from going to that country. And it can order the soldiers to stop any trains, automobiles, or trucks from going into that country.

This is like imposing sanctions against that country, to prevent coal, gasoline, guns, and other things from going to it. But if sanctions had not stopped those things from going in, a blockade would stop them.

Finally, the UN can order its forces to attack.

While the UN is staging "demonstrations" or imposing a blockade or sending soldiers and bombers, it must go right on recommending and persuading and talking things over. Even when this action is successful and the trouble-making nation stops, the UN still has to keep on recommending and persuading until the quarrel is really settled.

But it cannot use force to make a nation accept these recommendations. The UN can use force only to stop fights.

Suppose Egypt or some other nation is training a million soldiers, and its newspapers keep saying that it will conquer its neighbor. The Security Council or the General Assembly could recommend that that army be cut down to one hundred thousand men. The government of the nation goes right on training a million men. At the same time the government jails everyone who says he believes in democracy, and the police stand by and smile and do nothing when hoodlums smash the shop windows of people whose religion is different from theirs and steal all the goods out of those shops.

The UN sends another message, saying, "We recommend that you cut down your army to one hundred thousand men, let people who believe in democracy out of jail, stop the smashing of shops, and have a free election to let your people vote on whether your government is the kind they want." At the same time the UN sends battleships and bombers and stages a "demonstration."

This scares the men in the government. They send back a message: "We have cut down our army to three hundred thousand."

The UN replies, "You say you have cut down your army to three hundred thousand, but you are still keeping the other seven hundred thousand men in camps near the border, and you have not done any of the things we recommended." So the UN orders a blockade and stops all ships, trains, and trucks from entering that country.

Not being able to bring any coal or gasoline or wheat into the country, the men in the government decide to send another message, "We have cut down our army to three hundred thousand. The other seven hundred thousand have gone home. We are not going to cause any war."

The UN studies this new situation. The nation has not done any of the things that were recommended. But it has stopped threatening to cause a war.

In that case the UN has to call off the blockade of the

country and send home its members' battleships and bombers.

In June 1950 when a North Korean army lunged into South Korea the Security Council met a few hours later. Having no UN army, it "called on all member nations" to send forces to resist the attack. Much time was wasted getting the troops together, but sixteen nations did send them, backed by the support of fifty-three nations, and the U.S.A. was given the principal authority for directing them.

On October 29, 1956, in response to Egyptian threats, Israeli forces lunged into Egypt. Again meeting within a few hours, the Security Council considered a motion to call on both sides to cease fire and let the UN handle the case. On October 30 France and Great Britain vetoed this motion (they were sending forces of their own into Egypt).

In such a case the Security Council, by vote of any seven members, can call a General Assembly meeting (where there is no veto). The council did this the very next day.

In emergencies each nation in the assembly needs only one delegate, as each nation has only one vote. The assembly met on the first of November and by an overwhelming majority called on all four countries to cease fire, stop taking weapons into Egypt, and let the UN handle the case.

Since the UN had no army, the assembly on November 5 voted to create one, to be directed by General E. L. M. Burns, an employee of the Secretariat. The secretary general, accepting contributions of troops from several nations, assembled a UN Emergency Force, which began landing November 11, welcomed by the Egyptian government; whereupon the four nations withdrew their soldiers. After much negotiating, Israel agreed in February to pull its last troops out of Egypt if the UN force would guard Aqaba Gulf and the Gaza Strip. The UN troops were stationed there and would remain for many years.

At the same time—in October 1956—the U.S.A. asked the Security Council to call on the Soviet Union to stop its military actions against a popular uprising in Hungary. This proposal was vetoed by the Soviet Union. The General Assembly in November called on the Soviet Union to withdraw its troops. And in December, by fifty-five votes against eight, the assembly condemned the "violation of the Charter by the U.S.S.R. in depriving Hungary of its liberty." But no attempt was made to send UN troops there, as they would not have been welcomed by the Hungarian government.

In the summer of 1960 the government of the brand-new Congo Republic (with capital at Leopoldville) appealed to the UN for help. The Congolese army had mutinied, one of its provinces tried to secede, and an army of foreign mercenaries threatened. This time the Security Council assumed responsibility for the case, while the UN sent in 20,000 soldiers (mostly from African countries), but as usual it was the General Assembly that voted the money for this undertaking.

The UN force did a great deal of negotiating, trying to

avoid battles, but was engaged in some fighting. And when the UN force withdrew, more than 1,000 civilians remained to help the war-torn country build itself up.

U Thant emphasized that the UN does not attempt to work miracles. In Cyprus he threatened to remove the UN force entirely if the local people would not cooperate with it, for, he said, he was not interested in "killing Cypriotes to prevent them from killing one another." This explains the difference between Hungary and the Congo. The UN never does anything in any country if the local government is not willing.

In 1963 the four Scandinavian countries and the Netherlands offered to keep "stand-by" military units for use in the UN's peace-keeping work. The secretary general, accepting these offers, said he hoped that many countries, especially the small ones, would do the same. If so, the original plan in the Charter would begin to be a reality.

Mr. Thant emphasized that when these groups of soldiers were not being used for UN work, they are not paid for by the UN and are not a UN force at all. In an emergency they can within a few hours become a UN force.

Recruiting the soldiers for this new kind of work, the Swedish government discovered that they would need a new kind of training. They would not try to conquer any country. Their duties would be to stop rioting mobs, to find and protect power houses, radio stations, and telephone exchanges, and to prevent fights. They would shoot, if necessary, only in self-defense.

Two battalions of volunteers were equipped, therefore, with small arms and rapid vehicles. A contingent of specialists was trained to operate public utilities and to guard city water supplies. And the government decided to prepare them also to give aid in earthquakes, hurricanes, and floods. An air transport group began practicing with helicopters and other planes able to land on small fields.

These volunteers have to keep up their vaccinations and their shots against cholera and typhus, and arrange with their employers and landlords for sudden departure in time of need.

Men began arriving from all round the world seeking these positions, for many are eager to help. Although the work is complex, dangerous, and very difficult, a lot of young people want to do it.

In the 1956 Suez crisis twenty-four nations offered soldiers for the UN force. Ten of these nations were asked to send them. In the Congo the UN troops were supplied voluntarily by ten countries, mostly African. And it became an educational experience for some persons in Leopoldville to see a police patrol of soldiers from Ethiopia, Ghana, Ireland, and Sweden.

This voluntary method may be by far the best.

Money for these undertakings became a hard problem. In November 1950 the General Assembly (in the "uniting for peace resolutions") announced that in any crisis when the Security Council was held up by a veto, the assembly could be called together at once and would make "appropriate recommendations to the members for collective measures." So far, so good. The Charter says (Article 10) that the assembly can recommend pretty freely. Only Article 12 says the assembly must not contradict what the council is doing. But how about when the council is not doing anything?

That still leaves the question of money. Article 17 says, "The expenses of the Organization shall be borne by the Members as apportioned by the General Assembly." But when soldiers are sent voluntarily by ten nations, on recommendation by either the council or the assembly, is that part of "the expenses of the Organization"?

France and the Soviet Union have accepted only the first part of the "uniting for peace" resolution. In the Lebanon crisis of 1958 the U.S.A. and the U.S.S.R. together offered a motion to the Security Council calling for an emergency meeting of the General Assembly to deal with the case. This far the Russians were willing to go. But when the assembly asked all members to pay for military expenses, including the Suez and Congo operations, France and the Soviet Union refused.

Therefore the Cyprus work in 1964 was handled differently. The U.S.A. voluntarily gave some of the money. Cyprus itself pledged $280,000. Switzerland, though not a member of the UN at all, contributed $75,000. Others made up the balance of what was needed.

Chapter 12

DISARMING THE NATIONS AND CONTROLLING THE ATOMIC BOMB

EVERY GOVERNMENT of every nation has always said, "We need an army for two reasons: first, to keep peace at home—if anybody here tries to start a revolution or if big mobs cause more trouble than our police can handle, we need an army to help make our people behave; second, to protect us if any other nation attacks us."

Sometimes there is a third reason: if they have an army they can go to war and conquer other lands.

But armies and weapons are expensive. They cost the world billions of dollars every year. When that money is taken out of the people's pockets (as taxes) and is spent on guns, bullets, and bombs, the people have just that much less to spend on food, clothes, houses, schools, swimming pools that would make their lives pleasanter and more comfortable. All the people in the world, including yourself and all your friends, are a lot poorer than you would be if your money did not go to pay for armies and weapons. That is what Article 26 of the Charter is about.

Also, weapons are dangerous. People who have guns sometimes become angry and are tempted to point them at somebody. When the men in a government know they have a powerful army, they often become impatient and are tempted to use it to take advantage of other nations.

If one nation gets a new kind of fighter plane, the next nation feels it needs a new kind of fighter plane, too. One nation gets an improved kind of flame thrower; so the next nation wants the same thing or a better one. This is what is called an "armaments race," in which each nation spends tremendous amounts of money trying to get ahead of the others.

And now both the United States and the Soviet Union have hydrogen bombs powerful enough to destroy whole continents. England, France, and China have atomic bombs.

Can we change armed nations into unarmed nations? If the governments really mean the promise they have signed (Article 2, paragraph 4) never to use force to try to conquer any land anywhere, that promise gets rid of the third reason for having an army.

If the UN is successful and really does save nations from being attacked, they will no longer have the second reason. They will need only a few soldiers and weapons to aid the UN in keeping peace.

That will leave only the first reason: to prevent revolutions and keep order at home. If a government is run in such a way that its own people are not starving and do have a chance to say what they please and to find jobs if they want to, that government does not need to fear revolutions or large disorders and does not need more than a militia of the kind we call the "national guard."

The Charter, therefore, says three times that the UN must try to get all governments to spend less money on weapons.

The first assembly began the big job of preparing general rules for disarming the world.

The Security Council, with the assistance of the Military Staff Committee, studied this problem and tried to prepare a definite plan.

If the big nations could agree on a program, the Security Council could put pressure behind it. The council might say to any small nations who refused it, "Watch out! If you don't accept this disarmament plan, your weapons may look like a threat to peace. And if we decide that they are, do you realize what the Charter says we can do to you?"

The problem is to get the big nations to agree on a good plan. In 1947 a special committee of the Security Council wrote one. It said the UN should create a commission or agency or authority of some sort to regulate all weapons for war. This UN agency would decide how many tanks and cannon and battleships each nation should keep ready for the UN to use. The agency should send inspectors to see that no nation had any other weapons. And the UN should immediately punish any nation that kept any extra weapons.

It was a bold plan. But the Big Five nations were not all ready to accept it.

The General Assembly created an Atomic Energy Commission to study the problem. The United States offered this Commission an even bolder plan, suggesting an Authority such as our quarrelsome world has never yet seen.

This Authority would be stronger than any nation. It was to be an *International Atomic Development Authority* composed of representatives of many nations. Each member would have one vote, and no country would have any veto power.

The Authority would own or control every factory where uranium or other fissionable materials are produced, and it would own or control all the dangerous stuff that comes out of those factories. And it would make laws, saying who could use these materials.

The key to the Authority's power would be very simple. Any person who should break its laws could be arrested and punished.

Notice this difference: According to the United Nations Charter, the UN can punish a whole nation but not individuals. This plan would give it the power to punish any guilty person.

The majority of the members of the Atomic Energy Commission were in favor of this plan. But obviously it would take away some of each nation's sovereign right to do as it pleased.

A large majority of the nations in the General Assembly voted (November 23, 1949) that that is just what is needed. Nations must give up some of their sovereignty to a UN agency which would manage fissionable material. But the big nations could not all agree to do so.

And now, although the Military Staff Committee meets in private, hints have leaked out that it is again at work on disarmament plans. The UN Disarmament Commission, with delegates from all member nations, is attacking the problem from the worldwide point of view. The Economic and Social Council has pursued intensive studies on what may happen to jobs and trade if the big nations begin to spend less on weapons. All these efforts supplement the frequent meetings of the seventeen-nation UN Disarmament Commission.

Chapter 13

HOW THE UN CAN BE CHANGED

ARE YOU satisfied with the UN as it is now? Do you think it does all it should? Can it do enough to make life pleasanter and more comfortable for people everywhere? Is it able to save us all from dying in an atomic war?

We, the people of the world, can change the Charter to say anything we want it to, by adding amendments.

Anybody can suggest an amendment. Any council or commission of the organization can recommend one. You can write to your country's representatives, telling them what changes you think they should vote for. Any nation can propose one.

Then the Charter gives two ways by which an amendment can go on from there. One way is for it to be discussed by the General Assembly, which may change it and improve it. Since all the member nations have representatives in the General Assembly, they should know which amendments the nations would probably accept and which ones they would certainly reject.

The other way is for the nations to send delegates to a big, special amending conference. Such a conference might be able to study proposed amendments in more detail than the assembly could.

When the General Assembly or the special conference has approved any amendment, copies are sent to all the governments, which are asked to ratify it. It is "ratified" by a nation when the government officially accepts it. In the United States the approval of two thirds of the Senate is required.

When an amendment has been ratified by two thirds of the member nations, including all the Big Five, it becomes part of the Charter of the United Nations. If the amendment contradicts some other sentence in the Charter, the old sentence does not count and the amendment does.

If one of the Big Five nations refuses to ratify a proposed amendment, it cannot be added to the Charter.

Because the number of members was almost doubled in the years 1955 to 1963, the General Assembly then voted (97 for and 11 against) to enlarge the Security Council by adding four more elective member nations to it. The assembly also voted (96 for and 11 against) to enlarge the Economic and Social Council by adding nine member nations to it.

But in the decision on each of these proposed amendments all the Big Five nations either voted against or abstained. So the chances of adoption were slim. Nevertheless, some such development seems inevitable eventually.

Strangely, in all the rather lengthy plan for UN military forces (Articles 43 to 48) the Charter says nothing about who shall pay for them. Therefore the UN has had serious difficulty collecting money for some of its undertakings, especially in Suez and in the Congo.

Also, its program of technical assistance to developing countries has been cramped by limited funds.

The UN has no power to force nations to pay. It cannot tax anyone. In its financial problem it resembles dramatically the so-called "United States" which in 1787 went bankrupt. The Articles of Confederation, like the UN Charter, did not give its organization any power to collect money. Therefore a group of delegates from the various states wrote the U.S. Constitution that summer, and the voters accepted it, making the states really united under a central government. The so-called "United Nations" cannot become really united or financially strong without a similar change.

The first ten amendments to the United States Constitution promised freedom of speech, freedom of religion, trial by jury, and other rights to all our citizens. The Commission on Human Rights of the United Nations may prepare some amendments to the UN Charter giving the International Court of Justice power to guarantee those rights to everyone in the world.

In the history of the League of Nations the Big Five changed. Its Covenant named Great Britain, France, Italy, Japan, and the United States. As the United States failed to join, the League began with a Big Four. In 1926 Germany came in, making a Big Five. In 1934 the Soviet Union joined, making a Big Six.

What nations might change the UN similarly?

We might alter the way our representatives are chosen. Even in the United States, at first senators were not elected by the people; they were appointed by the legislatures of the states. In 1904 Oregon decided to let the voters elect them instead. Other states soon did the same. By 1910 the senators of three fourths of the states were being elected by the people instead of by the legislatures. Three years later an amendment was added to the Constitution of the United States saying that all senators must be elected.

Perhaps the United Nations will grow up the same way. Now the representatives in the General Assembly are appointed by the governments of the nations they come from. Those from the United States are appointed by the President. If they were elected by the voters perhaps the people would have more confidence in them.

Congress could decide to let the voters elect them. This would not require an amendment to the Charter. Other nations may do the same. And then some day an amendment might be added to the Charter saying that all representatives in the General Assembly must be elected. Already the British government has proposed this plan officially.

Delegates from Ecuador and from the Philippines have said the Charter should be amended to give the General Assembly the power to make laws. Some senators have spoken in favor of this idea. This would mean, for example, that the assembly could forbid any nation to draft young men for military training in peacetime or make any other preparations for large-scale war.

Many people are saying the United Nations should be given the power to arrest and punish any man who tries to cause a war. An amendment to the Charter could give it this power.

For U Thant has called the UN "our best hope for creating the beginnings of a civilized international community."

Chapter 14

A WORD OF WARNING

Two shipwrecked men were washed up on a deserted shore. When they had rested a little and were able to walk, they explored the land eagerly, only to discover that it was round, for it was an island. Then they were heavy at heart. The wind blew, rain fell upon them, and at night the island was cold.

Hurriedly they set to work building houses, each for himself. But it was hard, because one man could scarcely lift a beam alone.

When they searched for food for their stomachs, they worked hard again, for there was not enough. They grabbed whatever they could find and stuffed it into their mouths. One even seized some tiny fish out of a stream and ate them raw. The other cried out at him, "You are a savage!"

The first grew very angry but said nothing.

When at last they had time to look about a little, they

found they both were poor, having nothing but the work of their hands. The second man tried to make himself feel less ragged. He gathered gay-colored birds' feathers from the beach and tied them round his head, thinking they made him handsome.

"You fool!" cried the first. "Look at you! What a fool you are!"

"I will not be called fool by a savage!" shouted the other furiously.

"I will not be called savage by a fool!" growled the first showing at last how angry he was.

Each rushed to the other's house and tore it down.

And they were heavy at heart, for the wind blew, rain fell upon them, and at night the island was cold.

Gradually their tempers cooled.

At last one set to work again to build himself a house, while the other stood watching. It was hard, because one man could scarcely lift a beam into place alone.

Then he called out, "Come help me! And I will help you build yours."

So they worked together. And it was easier. Soon they both had better houses than before.

"Let us always stand ready to help each other," said one. "Life will be better this way on our island. And you may eat your fish any way you want to. That is nothing to me."

"Very well," agreed the other. "And I will not think you are a fool no matter what you wear. If we are to be friends, we must accept one another."

Those two men are you and I, and the island is round because it is the world. And too many of us are poor, without enough food to eat or good clothes to wear. Fearing people who are different, each of us has been squandering his money on bombs with which to destroy the others.

Life can be better on our round island if we help one another to build houses. We cannot afford to go on tearing down for each other what little we have.

Part IV—FACTS AND DOCUMENTS

Chapter 15

WHICH NATIONS ARE MEMBERS

W<small>E SAY</small> that the United Nations is (not "are") determined to keep peace and raise the world's standard of living. The Charter also refers to it as the "Organization." We often call it "the UN," though the British usually say "the UNO" (United Nations Organization) and the French say "l'ONU" (Organization des Nations Unies).

The original members were the fifty-one countries at war against Germany or Japan in the Second World War. They all signed the Charter and became members when their governments ratified it.

When any other nation wants to join, its government must inform the secretary general that it is willing to make all the promises in the Charter.

This is a serious matter. Every nation that signs the Charter agrees to work for the ideals expressed in Article 1 and obey the principles of Article 2. It promises to settle its disputes by peaceful means and never use force to grab anything from anybody. It promises to help the Security Council carry out any decision. For instance, a member may be asked to help stop the sale of guns or oil to some aggressor nation. Every member also offers to keep ready some soldiers and weapons which it will send out, at the UN's call, to enforce a UN blockade or even to resist an armed attack anywhere in the world. It agrees to send copies of all its treaties to the Secretariat, to be printed so that anybody can see them. It promises to pay to the organization as much money as the General Assembly says it should. It promises to help the Economic and Social Council to do its work of making life freer and pleasanter for everyone. It promises (Article 1, paragraph 3) never to treat anyone badly because of his religion or race.

If at least seven members of the Security Council, including all the Big Five, then vote to admit that country, and at least two thirds of the General Assembly vote for it, it becomes a member of the United Nations.

If a nation asks to be admitted and is refused, it can wait a while and then ask again. Some asked several times.

By the end of 1963 sixty-two nations had been admitted this way, making the total membership one hundred and thirteen. Consequently the desks were all ripped out of the General Assembly hall and smaller ones put in, so that this large number could be fitted into the available space.

The only nations not yet in were Germany, Switzerland, Korea (divided in two), Vietnam (also divided in two), and some border states of Arabia. Also a small number of large colonies, and a large number of very small ones, had not yet achieved independence.

Guessing the future, the experts designed the new seating arrangement of the assembly hall to allow space for 126 desks.

The General Assembly voted a resolution in 1946 saying that Spain would not be admitted so long as General Franco was dictator there. However, the members soon felt differently, for in 1948 a large majority voted that the UN should be a world organization where all nations could discuss their differences, and not a mere club of our friends.

When China signed the Charter and became one of the Big Five in the Security Council, Chiang Kai-shek's party ruled that country. But he was promptly driven out to the island of Taiwan, where his government is called "nationalist China," and Mao Tse-tung's communist party controlled the mainland. Every year thereafter the UN voted on which of them should represent China in the UN. Although Mao's government many times received only a minority of the votes, the number in his favor gradually increased. After Great Britain and France both recognized his regime as the real government of China, it seemed probable that the General Assembly, by a two thirds majority, would soon admit his delegates in place of Chiang Kai-shek's.

If a nation wants to resign. There is nothing in the Charter about withdrawing from membership.

The Covenant of the League of Nations said that every member had the right to get out whenever it wanted to, regardless of whether it had a good reason. What actually happened was that every time the League criticized a nation for misbehaving, that nation immediately resigned from the League. When Germany wanted to conquer the world, it first resigned from the League.

It will not do a country any good to resign from the United Nations, because Article 2, paragraph 6, says the organization has just as much power over nonmembers as over members.

It says, however, that the Security Council and the General Assembly together can expel a member for bad behavior (Article 6).

Also, any nation that fails to pay its dues for two years can be deprived of its vote in the General Assembly (Article 19). Forty nations (including France and the Soviet Union) refused to pay their shares of the expenses in the Suez expedition or in the Congo, because some of the decisions were made in the General Assembly in a way that those nations said was illegal. Most paid enough to keep their votes, but some nations did not.

As their exclusion from voting in the assembly would be impractical and would settle nothing, a compromise became necessary. Ultimately the UN has no power to force any member nation to pay anything.

Chapter 16

SPECIAL AGENCIES FOR SPECIAL JOBS

THIS CHAPTER tells about specialized agencies of the UN that are already working. More have been planned.

UNESCO. The *United Nations Educational, Scientific, and Cultural Organization,* which began in League of Nations days, with Einstein and Mme Curie, as a meeting place for world-famous geniuses, developed a program to help universities and research laboratories work together.

It joined the UN on the theory that if nations are helped to understand one another, they will be less likely to fight.

But, in response to the UN's discovery that one quarter of the men and women in the world could not read or write, UNESCO came down from those lofty theories and began giving training courses to teachers who would teach illiterate adults. Prodded by the Economic and Social Council, this agency has been spending three million dollars

a year in the poorer countries for teachers' colleges, preparation of children's textbooks, and aid to libraries.

Unfortunately, as recently as 1960, in eighty-five underdeveloped countries, nearly half the children of school age were not in school. As these youngsters grow up, still with no education, the number of illiterate adults increases by more than twenty million every year.

In a huge new building in Paris delegates from member nations meet every other year. Nearly all countries in the world are members. They elect an executive board of twenty-four persons (all from different countries), who meet twice a year to direct the agency. And its own secretariat works all the time.

It is very large. In one typical month UNESCO played host to international conferences in eleven cities round the world all at once. Turning its scientific facilities to practical use, it runs institutes in Latin America and in the Near and Far East to apply science to immediate problems in field, factory, and mine.

UPU. The reliable old *Universal Postal Union*, which began in 1874 when the head of the United States Post Office talked a few other nations into working together, grew and grew, till it has far more members than there are free nations in the world. (It lets colonies in, since they need mail service, too.) And it joined up with the UN.

We are so used to the UPU that we can scarcely imagine how letters ever went from one country to another without it. In fact they went very haphazardly, until the UPU straightened out the ship and air mail routes and got the nations to agree on fair service. Now they all have promised that all letters will get the same efficient handling.

Its congress, with a vote for every member, meets once in five years, its committees more often. Its Secretariat (called "the Bureau"), at its headquarters in Berne, Switzerland, calculates each year how much each country owes for postal service, and sends out the bills.

ITU. Similarly the *International Telecommunication Union* has developed out of the old International Telegraph Union, which began in 1865. At first it recommended better laws about telegrams and got the nations to agree on much lower prices for sending a telegram from one country to another.

Later it added radio. It calls large conferences that decide what range of radio frequencies the stations in each country may use.

Then it added international telephones to its problems, and finally television.

And now it has joined up with the United Nations.

ICAO. If you travel far by air you notice that usually the police and customs inspections in different countries are simple and are much alike. They were not nearly so easy until the *International Civil Aviation Organization* helped the governments to straighten them out. Pilots and naviga-

tors notice even more the ICAO standard signal lights, radio beams, and traffic rules which most countries have adopted.

ICAO supports many technical-assistance projects, especially for training pilots and ground crews. For instance, the government of Indonesia, with ICAO help, established a National Aviation College.

ICAO's Council can even serve—like the Security Council—to settle disputes between nations. In a case between India and Pakistan it enabled them to arrange a plan whereby Indian aircraft could fly to Afghanistan and refuel at Kabul with gasoline sent there by Pakistan.

Headquarters are in Montreal, field offices in Lima, Paris, Cairo, Bangkok.

IMCO. Poorer countries, that send and receive goods on other peoples' ships, confer in meetings called by the *Intergovernmental Maritime Consultative Organization,* whose members include the big ship-owning nations. It has been fairly easy for them to agree on regulations for safety at sea, and even on proper conduct by shipping companies. But they bargain hard over the many regulations made by governments in the different countries. And on the big question of prices they really become angry.

Headquarters are in London.

FAO. The *Food and Agriculture Organization* was created at the end of the Second World War for two reasons. Many people were hungry. And many farmers complained that no matter how hard they worked, they could not make a living. Since both problems were world-wide, FAO soon had more member nations than the UN itself.

With its headquarters in Rome, its work is extended from its offices in Washington, Mexico City, Rio de Janeiro, Santiago de Chile, and in Cairo, Accra, Bangkok.

At its General Conference every other year each member nation has only one vote, but you can get some idea of how these agencies look from the fact that the U.S.A. has sent as many as twenty-seven delegates (four of them congressmen), plus eleven assistants, to one meeting. They have bargained repeatedly over the difficult question of food prices on the world market. For example, enormous quantities of American wheat are piled up in warehouses while Indians and Africans starve; but if we give away too much in one year, or sell it cheaply, the price will drop till wheat farmers in France and Argentina cannot earn a living. There must be a solution, if only the nations could agree.

FAO also calls international conferences for special purposes. It has invited delegates of many nations to meetings to discuss the improvement of rice farming, or sheep, cow, and milk production, or fisheries, or what to do about insects and rats in the food supply.

Recently FAO has stepped up its technical assistance to poorer countries. It sends an expert to show Afghan farmers how to raise larger crops, or Philippine communities how to drain swamps. But that is not enough. So it is work-

ing harder and harder on colleges that teach local government officials all that is known about livestock improvement, the use of radio isotopes on farms, how to improve
laws on fish and farm markets, and on supplying meals to
school children.

FAO finds the teachers, pays for equipment, manages
the programs. The local governments supply the buildings
where the teaching is done, find the students, and pay the
salaries. Usually the government receiving this help pays
more than FAO or the UN does.

WMO. When nations found that they were not getting
enough cooperation from one another on weather reports,
they created an international weather bureau in 1878. By
1950 it had become so large, and weather predicting had
changed so much, that the bureau was reorganized as the
World Meteorological Organization and joined the UN.

Ships, airplanes, electric companies, farmers have benefit-
ted from its discovery that weather ignores national boun-

daries. In the brand-new nation of Libya WMO experts helped the government set up a national weather service. Other new nations soon needed them, too. This agency has helped several countries to build windmills for generating electricity out in deserts, where there is plenty of wind and very little else.

WHO. Public health departments of nearly all countries are represented in the *World Health Organization.*

Several countries, where too many people were catching malaria, asked WHO for help. The agency sent a team of specialists to show what could be done against malaria-carrying mosquitoes. Results have been surprising. Farm areas in some parts of Greece began producing double the crops they used to. Investigators found this happened simply because at harvest time so many farmers were in the fields instead of sick in bed. In Afghanistan the textile mills turned out twice as much cloth because the workers were on the job instead of at home with fever.

WHO, working with the UN Children's Fund, tackled typhus in Guatemala. Typhus cases dropped from over 2,800 in 1945 to exactly 8 cases in 1951.

WHO oversees medical research and collects information, which is welcomed and used by government health officers and heads of hospitals nearly everywhere. Now no country needs to be out of touch with modern hygiene and new medical discoveries.

In poor countries where many young men and women cannot find a good medical school WHO gives traveling

fellowships. Each year it enables several hundred people to study and do research in good colleges far from home. The purpose is to relieve the shortage of nurses and doctors.

IAEA. The U.S.A., which had loaned fissionable materials to thirty-five nations, served notice that they all must let their factories and laboratories using this stuff be inspected by experts from the UN's *International Atomic Energy Agency.*

Founded in 1957, the IAEA is becoming the world's police agency to guarantee that uranium and other fissionable elements intended for peaceful purposes do not get used for bombs.

Its general conference meets each year, with one vote for every member nation, including the U.S.A. and the U.S.S.R. Its Board of Governors (consisting of delegates from twenty-three nations) meets more often. The headquarters are in Vienna.

Can you think of anything else this agency might do?

ILO. How can the nations trade freely with one another if shoes, ladies' dresses, and portable radios are made in some places by men and women earning two or three dollars an hour, and the same things are being made elsewhere by men and women earning only ten cents an hour? The ideal of the *International Labor Organization* has been to raise the pay of workers in poor countries until they will not offer unfair competition with workers in richer countries.

ILO has an unusual form of organization. In its annual general conference every member nation has four votes, two cast by delegates representing the government, one by a representative of employers and one by a labor union leader. (They often vote against each other.)

ILO tries to help workers to get good pay and decent, comfortable conditions in which to work. It tries to get all countries to pass laws saying that children must not be hired to do work that will ruin their health, that a working-man who is injured while working must be given proper medical care, and it helps governments arrange for unemployed workers to receive insurance money.

One of its biggest jobs lately has been technical assistance to help a factory produce more tractors or refrigerators, a coal mine more coal, a cotton mill more cloth. It sends workers to another country to see how the job is done so they can go back and teach their fellows. It sends an expert to work with the head of a plant or with the foremen in a shop, showing them more efficient methods. It often has nearly three hundred such projects going at once.

The *FUND* and *WORLD BANK* have headquarters in one building in Washington, along with the bank's two offshoots, the *IDA* and *IFC*. Since everyone needs money, they are very large, with more than a hundred member nations. Their annual meeting can be held anywhere, and it is impressive. In 1964 it was held in Tokyo, attended by 2,000 bankers and government officials who did a great deal besides talk. Between sessions Turkey's chief delegate (for instance) arranged a contract with Japan, which sells telephones to Turkey.

Backed at first by eight billion dollars supplied by its members, the *International Monetary Fund* helps the government of each nation to stabilize its currency, so that if a British pound is worth a certain number of dollars or a certain number of francs today, it will be worth the same number of dollars or francs six months later, and not keep sliding up and down. This stability makes it much easier for people to pay for anything they buy from another country.

Also, a company in Venezuela may sell large quantities

of oil to people in France, Italy, India. Suppose they don't have any Venezuelan money with which to pay for it. The Venezuelans say, "All right. Give us dollars." But those people may not have dollars either. The fund helps France, Italy, and India to exchange some of their money for Venezuelan money in order to keep the oil flowing.

Thus people buy more, and there is more world trade. The system has worked so well that the nations have voluntarily put more money into it, doubling the fund's cash resources.

The *Bank for Reconstruction and Development* is backed by over nine billion dollars, pledged by the countries that have joined. It lends money to help these countries build electric power plants and railroads or to buy locomotives, ships, passenger planes.

Many countries have been poor because they did not have factories to make plows or tools, telephones or wire, nor electric power to run such factories, nor roads or railroads to transport the goods.

When a country wants a loan from this bank, first the government prepares a plan showing what they intend to do. If the directors of the bank believe the purpose is really useful and the plan is good enough, they lend the money.

Then the bank offers businessmen all over the world a chance to buy some of the bank's own bonds.

India, for instance, created a committee to plow a large area of waste, deserted land where heavy kans grass prevented any crops from growing. After writing a plan, the committee borrowed money from the bank, bought trac-

tors and plows. Soon curved steel blades were ripping up the heavy grass, converting thousands of acres into farms.

IDA. Some of the less developed countries have turned to the *International Development Association.* Though run by the bank, it can make loans on easier terms, in order to give a boost to poorer countries.

IFC. Private enterprises can borrow from the *International Finance Corporation.* Though also run entirely by the bank, it can invest in useful industrial companies and give advice to their managers. It loaned, for instance, 2 million dollars to a new sugar company in Tanganyika.

Unfortunately these two agencies have had very limited resources.

Although the fund, the bank and the bank's two off-shoots take some risks, they have in fact cost their members nothing, because the bank has been operating ever since 1945 at a small profit.

Several attempts have been made to create a UN agency

for world trade, to work especially on the problems of tariff barriers and the regulation of prices. When poor countries try to sell coffee, cocoa, or tin and buy automobiles, plows, and electric motors, a hundred obstacles prevent them. Meanwhile the Economic and Social Council and its commissions have called delegates of the nations together repeatedly in large conferences where these trade problems are discussed and where some agreements are achieved.

Each specialized agency, in joining up with the UN, has promised to cooperate in many matters. It sends its own delegates to observe and sometimes talk in council and committee meetings of the UN. And it accepts delegates from the UN at its meetings.

In structure they follow one pattern. Experience has shown that it works. Each specialized agency is controlled by a big general conference or assembly, in which every member nation has one vote. Usually this meets every other year. It decides in general what the agency will do.

The delegates also elect a council or executive board of representatives from about twenty nations, who meet perhaps twice a year and direct the work.

And they hire a secretariat, which actually does the work. Each agency has its own director-general and a staff of clerks, research workers, experts. FAO employs about one thousand, some less.

Though each has its own headquarters in Geneva, Rome, London, or elsewhere, they all have offices, too, in the main UN building. So you can write to any of them at this address: United Nations, N.Y.

When these agencies began, many people believed they would merely gather and hand out information, and perhaps play host to international meetings for an exchange of ideas. Instead, the problem of poverty all round the world, which has grown worse each year, has forced them to turn more and more to real help for the hundreds of millions who are hungry, miserable, and desperate.

At the UN's Geneva Conference in 1964 the chief Nigerian delegate said, "You in the West tell us to work harder and we will get rich. Well, we are working hard, and we are getting poorer."

In these great conferences the UN and its agencies have made possible more and more agreements among the nations on the changes that are needed.

The UN and its agencies also give help directly.

Often several work together. ILO, for instance, assembled experts of its own and also some from FAO, UNESCO, and WHO, and they went and lived for a while in villages in the cold Andes Mountains to learn what the shepherds and farmers there really needed. The ILO men studied their working conditions and pay. The FAO men looked at their plows and seed. The UNESCO men visited schools and took a census to see how many adults could read. One of the WHO men was a doctor and was so busy he scarcely had time to sleep. Together they tackled questions such as, were the farmers poor because their plows were wrong or because their landlords got too much rent?

Showing how these projects are financed, the UN spent 2.8 million dollars and the Congolese government 7.8 million dollars to train Congolese men and women in two new institutes (like colleges), one for mining technicians, the other for junior high school teachers. The Congo government supplied the buildings and aided the students, while UNESCO sent the instructors and the books.

The UN, with a fund contributed voluntarily by a hundred nations, also gives fellowships to people of the poorer countries to go and study abroad. About two thousand fellowships a year are being given. The recipient governments are asked to choose persons as nearly as possible ready for important jobs; these should be taught first.

On request the UN sends experts to manage a government bank, head the public education department, or operate an airport for anywhere from a few months to a few years, while persons of that nation are being trained to do this work.

UN teams survey a developing country's resources: its land for farming, its rivers for electric power dams, its underground ores for mining. But every country's most important resources are its people. When the people have a chance to learn skills, the nation has a chance to improve its life.

Chapter 17

INTERNATIONAL AGREEMENTS

THE ATLANTIC CHARTER

The President of the United States of America and the Prime Minister, Mr. Churchill, representing his Majesty's Government in the United Kingdom, being met together, deem it right to make known certain common principles in the national policies of their respective countries on which they base their hopes for a better future for the world.

1. Their countries seek no aggrandizement, territorial or other.

2. They desire to see no territorial changes that do not accord with the freely expressed wishes of the peoples concerned.

3. They respect the right of all peoples to choose the form of government under which they will live; and they wish to see sovereign rights and self-government restored to those who have been forcibly deprived of them.

4. They will endeavor, with due respect for their existing obligations, to further the enjoyment by all States, great or small, victor or vanquished, of access, on equal terms, to the trade and to the raw materials of the world which are needed for their economic prosperity.

5. They desire to bring about the fullest collaboration between all nations in the economic field with the object of securing, for all,

improved labor standards, economic advancement and social security.

6. After the final destruction of the Nazi tyranny, they hope to see established a peace which will afford to all nations the means of dwelling in safety within their own boundaries, and which will afford assurance that all the men in all the lands may live out their lives in freedom from fear and want.

7. Such a peace should enable all men to traverse the high seas and oceans without hindrance.

8. They believe that all of the nations of the world, for realistic as well as spiritual reasons, must come to the abandonment of the use of force. Since no future peace can be maintained if land, sea or air armaments continue to be employed by nations which threaten, or may threaten, aggression outside of their frontiers, they believe, pending the establishment of a wider and permanent system of general security, that the disarmament of such nations is essential. They will likewise aid and encourage all other practicable measures which will lighten for peace-loving peoples the crushing burden of armaments.

FRANKLIN D. ROOSEVELT.
WINSTON S. CHURCHILL.

August 14, 1941.

DECLARATION BY UNITED NATIONS

A joint declaration by the United States of America, the United Kingdom of Great Britain and Northern Ireland, the Union of Soviet Socialist Republics, China, Australia, Belgium, Canada, Costa Rica, Cuba, Czechoslovakia, Dominican Republic, El Salvador, Greece, Guatemala, Haiti, Honduras, India, Luxembourg, Netherlands, New Zealand, Nicaragua, Norway, Panama, Poland, South Africa, Yugoslavia.

The governments signatory hereto,

Having subscribed to a common program of purposes and principles embodied in the joint declaration of the President of the United States of America and the Prime Minister of the United Kingdom of Great Britain and Northern Ireland dated August 14, 1941, known as the Atlantic Charter, being convinced that complete victory over their enemies is essential to defend life, liberty, independence and religious freedom, and to preserve human rights and justice in their own lands as well as in other lands, and that they are now engaged in a common struggle against savage and brutal forces seeking to subjugate the world, declare:

(1) Each government pledges itself to employ its full resources, military or economic, against those members of the tripartite pact and its adherents with which such government is at war.

(2) Each government pledges itself to co-operate with the governments signatory hereto and not to make a separate armistice or peace with the enemies.

The foregoing declaration may be adhered to by other nations which are, or which may be, rendering material assistance and contributions in the struggle for victory over Hitlerism.

Done at Washington.
January First, 1942.

CHARTER OF THE UNITED NATIONS

PREAMBLE

We the peoples of the United Nations determined

to save succeeding generations from the scourge of war, which twice in our lifetime has brought untold sorrow to mankind, and

to reaffirm faith in fundamental human rights, in the dignity and worth of the human person, in the equal rights of men and women and of nations large and small, and to establish conditions under which justice and respect for the obligations arising from treaties and other sources of international law can be maintained, and

to promote social progress and better standards of life in larger freedom,

and for these ends

to practice tolerance and live together in peace with one another as good neighbors, and

to unite our strength to maintain international peace and security, and

to ensure, by the acceptance of principles and the institution of methods, that armed force shall not be used, save in the common interest, and

to employ international machinery for the promotion of the economic and social advancement of all peoples,

have resolved to combine our efforts to accomplish these aims.

Accordingly, our respective Governments, through representatives assembled in the city of San Francisco, who have exhibited their full powers found to be in good and due form, have agreed to the present Charter of the United Nations and do hereby establish an international organization to be known as the United Nations.

CHAPTER I

PURPOSES AND PRINCIPLES

Article 1

The Purposes of the United Nations are:

1. To maintain international peace and security, and to that end:

to take effective collective measures for the prevention and removal of threats to the peace, and for the suppression of acts of aggression or other breaches of the peace, and to bring about by peaceful means, and in conformity with the principles of justice and international law, adjustment or settlement of international disputes or situations which might lead to a breach of the peace;

2. To develop friendly relations among nations based on respect for the principle of equal rights and self-determination of peoples, and to take other appropriate measures to strengthen universal peace;

3. To achieve international cooperation in solving international problems of an economic, social, cultural, or humanitarian character, and in promoting and encouraging respect for human rights and for fundamental freedoms for all without distinction as to race, sex, language, or religion; and

4. To be a center for harmonizing the actions of nations in the attainment of these common ends.

Article 2

The Organization and its Members, in pursuit of the Purposes stated in Article 1, shall act in accordance with the following Principles.

1. The Organization is based on the principle of the sovereign equality of all its Members.

2. All Members, in order to ensure to all of them the rights and benefits resulting from membership, shall fulfil in good faith the obligations assumed by them in accordance with the present Charter.

3. All Members shall settle their international disputes by peaceful means in such a manner that international peace and security, and justice are not endangered.

4. All Members shall refrain in their international relations from the threat or use of force against the territorial integrity or political

independence of any state, or in any other manner inconsistent with the Purposes of the United Nations.

5. All Members shall give the United Nations every assistance in any action it takes in accordance with the present Charter, and shall refrain from giving assistance to any state against which the United Nations is taking preventive or enforcement action.

6. The Organization shall ensure that states which are not Members of the United Nations act in accordance with these Principles so far as may be necessary for the maintenance of international peace and security.

7. Nothing contained in the present Charter shall authorize the United Nations to intervene in matters which are essentially within the domestic jurisdiction of any state or shall require the Members to submit such matters to settlement under the present Charter; but this principle shall not prejudice the application of enforcement measures under Chapter VII.

CHAPTER II

MEMBERSHIP

Article 3

The original Members of the United Nations shall be the states which, having participated in the United Nations Conference on International Organization at San Francisco, or having previously signed the Declaration by United Nations of January 1, 1942, sign the present Charter and ratify it in accordance with Article 110.

Article 4

1. Membership in the United Nations is open to all other peaceloving states which accept the obligations contained in the present Charter and, in the judgment of the Organization, are able and willing to carry out these obligations.

2. The admission of any such state to membership in the United Nations will be effected by a decision of the General Assembly upon the recommendation of the Security Council.

Article 5

A Member of the United Nations against which preventive or enforcement action has been taken by the Security Council may be suspended from the exercise of the rights and privileges of membership by the General Assembly upon the recommendation of the Security Council. The exercise of these rights and privileges may be restored by the Security Council.

Article 6

A Member of the United Nations which has persistently violated the Principles contained in the present Charter may be expelled from the Organization by the General Assembly upon the recommendation of the Security Council.

CHAPTER III

ORGANS

Article 7

1. There are established as the principal organs of the United Nations: a General Assembly, a Security Council, an Economic and Social Council, a Trusteeship Council, an International Court of Justice, and a Secretariat.

2. Such subsidiary organs as may be found necessary may be established in accordance with the present Charter.

Article 8

The United Nations shall place no restrictions on the eligibility of men and women to participate in any capacity and under conditions of equality in its principal and subsidiary organs.

CHAPTER IV

THE GENERAL ASSEMBLY
COMPOSITION

Article 9

1. The General Assembly shall consist of all the Members of the United Nations.

2. Each Member shall have not more than five representatives in the General Assembly.

FUNCTIONS AND POWERS

Article 10

The General Assembly may discuss any questions or any matters within the scope of the present Charter or relating to the powers and functions of any organs provided for in the present Charter, and, except as provided in Article 12, may make recommendations to the Members of the United Nations or to the Security Council or to both on any such questions or matters.

Article 11

1. The General Assembly may consider the general principles of cooperation in the maintenance of international peace and security, including the principles governing disarmament and the regulation of armaments, and may make recommendations with regard to such principles to the Members or to the Security Council or to both.

2. The General Assembly may discuss any questions relating to the maintenance of international peace and security brought before

it by any Member of the United Nations, or by the Security Council, or by a state which is not a Member of the United Nations in accordance with Article 35, paragraph 2, and, except as provided in Article 12, may make recommendations with regard to any such questions to the state or states concerned or to the Security Council or to both. Any such question on which action is necessary shall be referred to the Security Council by the General Assembly either before or after discussion.

3. The General Assembly may call the attention of the Security Council to situations which are likely to endanger international peace and security.

4. The powers of the General Assembly set forth in this Article shall not limit the general scope of Article 10.

Article 12

1. While the Security Council is exercising in respect of any dispute or situation the functions assigned to it in the present Charter, the General Assembly shall not make any recommendation with regard to that dispute or situation unless the Security Council so requests.

2. The Secretary-General, with the consent of the Security Council, shall notify the General Assembly at each session of any matters relative to the maintenance of international peace and security which are being dealt with by the Security Council and shall similarly notify the General Assembly, or the Members of the United Nations if the General Assembly is not in session, immediately the Security Council ceases to deal with such matters.

Article 13

1. The General Assembly shall initiate studies and make recommendations for the purpose of:

(a) promoting international cooperation in the political field and encouraging the progressive development of international law and its codification;

(b) promoting international cooperation in the economic, social, cultural, educational, and health fields, and assisting in the realization of human rights and fundamental freedoms for all without distinction as to race, sex, language, or religion.

2. The further responsibilities, functions, and powers of the General Assembly with respect to matters mentioned in paragraph 1 (b) above are set forth in Chapters IX and X.

Article 14

Subject to the provisions of Article 12, the General Assembly may recommend measures for the peaceful adjustment of any situation, regardless of origin, which it deems likely to impair the general welfare or friendly relations among nations, including situations resulting from a violation of the provisions of the present Charter setting forth the Purposes and Principles of the United Nations.

Article 15

1. The General Assembly shall receive and consider annual and special reports from the Security Council; these reports shall include an account of the measures that the Security Council has decided upon or taken to maintain international peace and security.

2. The General Assembly shall receive and consider reports from the other organs of the United Nations.

Article 16

The General Assembly shall perform such functions with respect to the international trusteeship system as are assigned to it under Chapters XII and XIII, including the approval of the trusteeship agreements for areas not designated as strategic.

Article 17

1. The General Assembly shall consider and approve the budget of the Organization.

2. The expenses of the Organization shall be borne by the Members as apportioned by the General Assembly.

3. The General Assembly shall consider and approve any financial and budgetary arrangements with specialized agencies referred to in Article 57 and shall examine the administrative budgets of such specialized agencies with a view to making recommendations to the agencies concerned.

VOTING

Article 18

1. Each member of the General Assembly shall have one vote.

2. Decisions of the General Assembly on important questions shall be made by a two-thirds majority of the members present and voting. These questions shall include: recommendations with respect to the maintenance of international peace and security, the election of the non-permanent members of the Security Council, the election of the members of the Economic and Social Council, the election of members of the Trusteeship Council in accordance with paragraph 1 (c) of Article 86, the admission of new Members to the United Nations, the suspension of the rights and privileges of membership, the expulsion of Members, questions relating to the operation of the trusteeship system, and budgetary questions.

3. Decisions on other questions, including the determination of additional categories of questions to be decided by a two-thirds majority, shall be made by a majority of the members present and voting.

Article 19

A Member of the United Nations which is in arrears in the payment of its financial contributions to the Organization shall have no vote in the General Assembly if the amount of its arrears equals or exceeds the amount of the contributions due from it for the preceding two full years. The General Assembly may, nevertheless, permit such a Member to vote if it is satisfied that the failure to pay is due to conditions beyond the control of the Member.

PROCEDURE

Article 20

The General Assembly shall meet in regular annual sessions and in such special sessions as occasion may require. Special sessions shall be convoked by the Secretary-General at the request of the Security Council or of a majority of the Members of the United Nations.

Article 21

The General Assembly shall adopt its own rules of procedure. It shall elect its President for each session.

Article 22

The General Assembly may establish such subsidiary organs as it deems necessary for the performance of its functions.

CHAPTER V

THE SECURITY COUNCIL
COMPOSITION

Article 23

1. The Security Council shall consist of eleven Members of the United Nations. The Republic of China, France, the Union of

Soviet Socialist Republics, the United Kingdom of Great Britain and Northern Ireland, and the United States of America shall be permanent members of the Security Council. The General Assembly shall elect six other Members of the United Nations to be non-permanent members of the Security Council, due regard being specially paid, in the first instance to the contribution of Members of the United Nations to the maintenance of international peace and security and to the other purposes of the Organization, and also to equitable geographical distribution.

2. The non-permanent members of the Security Council shall be elected for a term of two years. In the first election of the non-permanent members, however, three shall be chosen for a term of one year. A retiring member shall not be eligible for immediate re-election.

3. Each member of the Security Council shall have one representative.

FUNCTIONS AND POWERS

Article 24

1. In order to ensure prompt and effective action by the United Nations, its Members confer on the Security Council primary responsibility for the maintenance of international peace and security, and agree that in carrying out its duties under this responsibility the Security Council acts on their behalf.

2. In discharging these duties the Security Council shall act in accordance with the Purposes and Principles of the United Nations. The specific powers granted to the Security Council for the discharge of these duties are laid down in Chapters VI, VII, VIII, and XII.

3. The Security Council shall submit annual and, when necessary, special reports to the General Assembly for its consideration.

Article 25

The Members of the United Nations agree to accept and carry out the decisions of the Security Council in accordance with the present Charter.

Article 26

In order to promote the establishment and maintenance of international peace and security with the least diversion for armaments of the world's human and economic resources, the Security Council shall be responsible for formulating, with the assistance of the Military Staff Committee referred to in Article 47, plans to be submitted to the Members of the United Nations for the establishment of a system for the regulation of armaments.

VOTING

Article 27

1. Each member of the Security Council shall have one vote.

2. Decisions of the Security Council on procedural matters shall be made by an affirmative vote of seven members.

3. Decisions of the Security Council on all other matters shall be made by an affirmative vote of seven members including the concurring votes of the permanent members; provided that, in decisions under Chapter VI, and under paragraph 3 of Article 52, a party to a dispute shall abstain from voting.

PROCEDURE

Article 28

1. The Security Council shall be so organized as to be able to

function continuously. Each member of the Security Council shall for this purpose be represented at all times at the seat of the Organization.

2. The Security Council shall hold periodic meetings at which each of its members may, if it so desires, be represented by a member of the government or by some other specially designated representative.

3. The Security Council may hold meetings at such places other than the seat of the Organization as in its judgment will best facilitate its work.

Article 29

The Security Council may establish such subsidiary organs as it deems necessary for the performance of its functions.

Article 30

The Security Council shall adopt its own rules of procedure, including the method of selecting its President.

Article 31

Any Member of the United Nations which is not a member of the Security Council may participate, without vote, in the discussion of any question brought before the Security Council whenever the latter considers that the interests of that Member are specially affected.

Article 32

Any Member of the United Nations which is not a member of the Security Council or any state which is not a Member of the United Nations, if it is a party to a dispute under consideration by the Security Council, shall be invited to participate, without vote, in the discussion relating to the dispute. The Security Council shall lay down such conditions as it deems just for the participation of a state which is not a Member of the United Nations.

CHAPTER VI

PACIFIC SETTLEMENT OF DISPUTES

Article 33

1. The parties to any dispute, the continuance of which is likely to endanger the maintenance of international peace and security, shall, first of all, seek a solution by negotiation, enquiry, mediation, conciliation, arbitration, judicial settlement, resort to regional agencies or arrangements, or other peaceful means of their own choice.

2. The Security Council shall, when it deems necessary, call upon the parties to settle their dispute by such means.

Article 34

The Security Council may investigate any dispute, or any situation which might lead to international friction or give rise to a dispute, in order to determine whether the continuance of the dispute or situation is likely to endanger the maintenance of international peace and security.

Article 35

1. Any Member of the United Nations may bring any dispute, or any situation of the nature referred to in Article 34, to the attention of the Security Council or of the General Assembly.

2. A state which is not a Member of the United Nations may bring to the attention of the Security Council or of the General Assembly any dispute to which it is a party if it accepts in advance,

for the purposes of the dispute, the obligations of pacific settlement provided in the present Charter.

3. The proceedings of the General Assembly in respect of matters brought to its attention under this Article will be subject to the provisions of Articles 11 and 12.

Article 36

1. The Security Council may, at any stage of a dispute of the nature referred to in Article 33 or of a situation of like nature, recommend appropriate procedures or methods of adjustment.

2. The Security Council should take into consideration any procedures for the settlement of the dispute which have already been adopted by the parties.

3. In making recommendations under this Article the Security Council should also take into consideration that legal disputes should as a general rule be referred by the parties to the International Court of Justice in accordance with the provisions of the Statute of the Court.

Article 37

1. Should the parties to a dispute of the nature referred to in Article 33 fail to settle it by the means indicated in that Article, they shall refer it to the Security Council.

2. If the Security Council deems that the continuance of the dispute is in fact likely to endanger the maintenance of international peace and security, it shall decide whether to take action under Article 36 or to recommend such terms of settlement as it may consider appropriate.

Article 38

Without prejudice to the provisions of Articles 33 to 37, the Security Council may, if all the parties to any dispute so request, make recommendations to the parties with a view to a pacific settlement of the dispute.

CHAPTER VII

ACTION WITH RESPECT TO THREATS TO THE PEACE, BREACHES OF THE PEACE AND ACTS OF AGGRESSION

Article 39

The Security Council shall determine the existence of any threat to the peace, breach of the peace, or act of aggression and shall make recommendations, or decide what measures shall be taken in accordance with Articles 41 and 42, to maintain or restore international peace and security.

Article 40

In order to prevent an aggravation of the situation, the Security Council may, before making the recommendations or deciding upon the measures provided for in Article 39, call upon the parties concerned to comply with such provisional measures as it deems necessary or desirable. Such provisional measures shall be without prejudice to the rights, claims, or position of the parties concerned. The Security Council shall duly take account of failure to comply with such provisional measures.

Article 41

The Security Council may decide what measures not involving the use of armed force are to be employed to give effect to its decisions, and it may call upon the Members of the United Nations to apply such measures. These may include complete or partial interruption of economic relations and of rail, sea, air, postal, telegraphic, radio, and other means of communication, and the severance of diplomatic relations.

Article 42

Should the Security Council consider that measures provided for in Article 41 would be inadequate or have proved to be inadequate, it may take such action by air, sea, or land forces as may be necessary to maintain or restore international peace and security. Such action may include demonstrations, blockade, and other operations by air, sea, or land forces of Members of the United Nations.

Article 43

1. All Members of the United Nations, in order to contribute to the maintenance of international peace and security, undertake to make available to the Security Council, on its call and in accordance with a special agreement or agreements, armed forces, assistance, and facilities, including rights of passage, necessary for the purpose of maintaining international peace and security.

2. Such agreement or agreements shall govern the numbers and types of forces, their degree of readiness and general location, and the nature of the facilities and assistance to be provided.

3. The agreement or agreements shall be negotiated as soon as possible on the initiative of the Security Council. They shall be concluded between the Security Council and Members or between the Security Council and groups of Members and shall be subject to ratification by the signatory states in accordance with their respective constitutional processes.

Article 44

When the Security Council has decided to use force it shall, before calling upon a Member not represented on it to provide armed forces in fulfillment of the obligations assumed under Article 43, invite that Member, if the Member so desires, to participate in the decisions of the Security Council concerning the employment of contingents of that Member's armed forces.

Article 45

In order to enable the United Nations to take urgent military measures, Members shall hold immediately available national air-force contingents for combined international enforcement action. The strength and degree of readiness of these contingents and plans for their combined action shall be determined, within the limits laid down in the special agreement or agreements referred to in Article 43, by the Security Council with the assistance of the Military Staff Committee.

Article 46

Plans for the application of armed force shall be made by the Security Council with the assistance of the Military Staff Committee.

Article 47

1. There shall be established a Military Staff Committee to advise and assist the Security Council on all questions relating to the Security Council's military requirements for the maintenance of international peace and security, the employment and command of forces placed at its disposal, the regulation of armaments, and possible disarmament.

2. The Military Staff Committee shall consist of the Chiefs of Staff of the permanent members of the Security Council or their representatives. Any Member of the United Nations not permanently represented on the Committee shall be invited by the Committee to be associated with it when the efficient discharge of the Committee's responsibilities requires the participation of that Member in its work.

3. The Military Staff Committee shall be responsible under the Security Council for the strategic direction of any armed forces placed at the disposal of the Security Council. Questions relating to the command of such forces shall be worked out subsequently.

4. The Military Staff Committee, with the authorization of the Security Council and after consultation with appropriate regional agencies, may establish regional subcommittees.

Article 48

1. The action required to carry out the decisions of the Security Council for the maintenance of international peace and security shall be taken by all the Members of the United Nations or by some of them, as the Security Council may determine.

2. Such decisions shall be carried out by the Members of the United Nations directly and through their action in the appropriate international agencies of which they are members.

Article 49

The Members of the United Nations shall join in affording mutual assistance in carrying out the measures decided upon by the Security Council.

Article 50

If preventive or enforcement measures against any state are taken by the Security Council, any other state, whether a Member of the United Nations or not, which finds itself confronted with special economic problems arising from the carrying out of those measures shall have the right to consult the Security Council with regard to a solution of those problems.

Article 51

Nothing in the present Charter shall impair the inherent right of individual or collective self-defense if an armed attack occurs against a Member of the United Nations, until the Security Council has taken the measures necessary to maintain international peace and security. Measures taken by Members in the exercise of this right of self-defense shall be immediately reported to the Security Council and shall not in any way affect the authority and responsibility of the Security Council under the present Charter to take at any time such action as it deems necessary in order to maintain or restore international peace and security.

CHAPTER VIII

REGIONAL ARRANGEMENTS

Article 52

1. Nothing in the present Charter precludes the existence of regional arrangements or agencies for dealing with such matters relating to the maintenance of international peace and security as are appropriate for regional action, provided that such arrangements or agencies and their activities are consistent with the Purposes and Principles of the United Nations.

2. The Members of the United Nations entering into such arrangements or constituting such agencies shall make every effort to achieve pacific settlement of local disputes through such regional arrangements or by such regional agencies before referring them to the Security Council.

3. The Security Council shall encourage the development of pacific settlement of local disputes through such regional arrangements or by such regional agencies either on the initiative of the states concerned or by reference from the Security Council.

4. This Article in no way impairs the application of Articles 34 and 35.

Article 53

1. The Security Council shall, where appropriate, utilize such regional arrangements or agencies for enforcement action under its authority. But no enforcement action shall be taken under regional arrangements or by regional agencies without the authorization of the Security Council, with the exception of measures against any enemy state, as defined in paragraph 2 of this Article, provided for

pursuant to Article 107 or in regional arrangements directed against renewal of aggressive policy on the part of any such state, until such time as the Organization may, on request of the Governments concerned, be charged with the responsibility for preventing further aggression by such a state.

2. The term enemy state as used in paragraph 1 of this Article applies to any state which during the Second World War has been an enemy of any signatory of the present Charter.

Article 54

The Security Council shall at all times be kept fully informed of activities undertaken or in contemplation under regional arrangements or by regional agencies for the maintenance of international peace and security.

CHAPTER IX

INTERNATIONAL ECONOMIC AND SOCIAL COOPERATION

Article 55

With a view to the creation of conditions of stability and well-being which are necessary for peaceful and friendly relations among nations based on respect for the principle of equal rights and self-determination of peoples, the United Nations shall promote:

(a) higher standards of living, full employment, and conditions of economic and social progress and development;

(b) solutions of international economic, social, health, and related problems; and international cultural and educational cooperation; and

(c) universal respect for, and observance of, human rights and fundamental freedoms for all without distinction as to race, sex, language, or religion.

Article 56

All Members pledge themselves to take joint and separate action in cooperation with the Organization for the achievement of the purposes set forth in Article 55.

Article 57

1. The various specialized agencies, established by intergovernmental agreement and having wide international responsibilities, as defined in their basic instruments, in economic, social, cultural, educational, health, and related fields, shall be brought into relationship with the United Nations in accordance with the provisions of Article 63.

2. Such agencies thus brought into relationship with the United Nations are hereinafter referred to as specialized agencies.

Article 58

The Organization shall make recommendations for the co-ordination of the policies and activities of the specialized agencies.

Article 59

The Organization shall, where appropriate, initiate negotiations among the states concerned for the creation of any new specialized agencies required for the accomplishment of the purposes set forth in Article 55.

Article 60

Responsibility for the discharge of the functions of the Organization set forth in this Chapter shall be vested in the General Assembly and, under the authority of the General Assembly, in the Economic and Social Council, which shall have for this purpose the powers set forth in Chapter X.

CHAPTER X

THE ECONOMIC AND SOCIAL COUNCIL
COMPOSITION

Article 61

1. The Economic and Social Council shall consist of eighteen Members of the United Nations elected by the General Assembly.

2. Subject to the provisions of paragraph 3, six members of the Economic and Social Council shall be elected each year for a term of three years. A retiring member shall be eligible for immediate re-election.

3. At the first election, eighteen members of the Economic and Social Council shall be chosen. The term of office of six members so chosen shall expire at the end of one year, and of six other members at the end of two years, in accordance with arrangements made by the General Assembly.

4. Each member of the Economic and Social Council shall have one representative.

FUNCTIONS AND POWERS

Article 62

1. The Economic and Social Council may make or initiate studies and reports with respect to international economic, social, cultural, educational, health, and related matters and may make recommendations with respect to any such matters to the General Assembly, to the Members of the United Nations, and to the specialized agencies concerned.

2. It may make recommendations for the purpose of promoting respect for, and observance of, human rights and fundamental freedoms for all.

3. It may prepare draft conventions for submission to the General Assembly, with respect to matters falling within its competence.

4. It may call, in accordance with the rules prescribed by the United Nations, international conferences on matters falling within its competence.

Article 63

1. The Economic and Social Council may enter into agreements with any of the agencies referred to in Article 57, defining the terms on which the agency concerned shall be brought into relationship with the United Nations. Such agreements shall be subject to approval by the General Assembly.

2. It may co-ordinate the activities of the specialized agencies through consultation with and recommendations to such agencies and through recommendations to the General Assembly and to Members of the United Nations.

Article 64

1. The Economic and Social Council may take appropriate steps to obtain regular reports from the specialized agencies. It may make arrangements with the Members of the United Nations and with the specialized agencies to obtain reports on the steps taken to give effect to its own recommendations and to recommendations on matters falling within its competence made by the General Assembly.

2. It may communicate its observations on these reports to the General Assembly.

Article 65

The Economic and Social Council may furnish information to the Security Council and shall assist the Security Council upon its request.

Article 66

1. The Economic and Social Council shall perform such functions as fall within its competence in connection with the carrying out of the recommendations of the General Assembly.

2. It may, with the approval of the General Assembly, perform services at the request of Members of the United Nations and at the request of specialized agencies.

3. It shall perform such other functions as are specified elsewhere in the present Charter or as may be assigned to it by the General Assembly.

VOTING

Article 67

1. Each member of the Economic and Social Council shall have one vote.

2. Decisions of the Economic and Social Council shall be made by a majority of the members present and voting.

PROCEDURE

Article 68

The Economic and Social Council shall set up commissions in economic and social fields and for the promotion of human rights, and such other commissions as may be required for the performance of its functions.

Article 69

The Economic and Social Council shall invite any Member of the United Nations to participate, without vote, in its deliberations on any matter of particular concern to that Member.

Article 70

The Economic and Social Council may make arrangements for representatives of the specialized agencies to participate, without vote, in its deliberations and in those of the commissions established by it, and for its representatives to participate in the deliberations of the specialized agencies.

Article 71

The Economic and Social Council may make suitable arrangements for consultation with non-governmental organizations which are concerned with matters within its competence. Such arrangements may be made with international organizations and, where appropriate, with national organizations after consultation with the Member of the United Nations concerned.

Article 72

1. The Economic and Social Council shall adopt its own rules of procedure, including the method of selecting its President.
2. The Economic and Social Council shall meet as required in accordance with its rules, which shall include provision for the convening of meetings on the request of a majority of its members.

CHAPTER XI

DECLARATION REGARDING NON-SELF-GOVERNING TERRITORIES

Article 73

Members of the United Nations which have or assume responsibilities for the administration of territories whose peoples have not yet attained a full measure of self-government recognize the princi-

ple that the interests of the inhabitants of these territories are paramount, and accept as a sacred trust the obligation to promote to the
utmost, within the system of international peace and security established by the present Charter, the well-being of the inhabitants of
these territories, and, to this end:

(a) to ensure, with due respect for the culture of the peoples
concerned, their political, economic, social, and educational advancement, their just treatment, and their protection against abuses;

(b) to develop self-government, to take due account of the political aspirations of the peoples, and to assist them in the progressive
development of their free political institutions, according to the
particular circumstances of each territory and its peoples and their
varying stages of advancement;

(c) to further international peace and security;

(d) to promote constructive measures of development, to encourage research, and to cooperate with one another and, when
and where appropriate, with specialized international bodies with
a view to the practical achievement of the social, economic, and
scientific purposes set forth in this Article; and

(e) to transmit regularly to the Secretary-General for information purposes, subject to such limitation as security and constitutional considerations may require, statistical and other information
of a technical nature relating to economic, social, and educational
conditions in the territories for which they are respectively responsible other than those territories to which Chapters XII and XIII
apply.

Article 74

Members of the United Nations also agree that their policy in
respect of the territories to which this Chapter applies, no less than
in respect of their metropolitan areas, must be based on the general
principle of good-neighborliness, due account being taken of the
interests and well-being of the rest of the world, in social, economic,
and commercial matters.

CHAPTER XII

INTERNATIONAL TRUSTEESHIP SYSTEM

Article 75

The United Nations shall establish under its authority an international trusteeship system for the administration and supervision of such territories as may be placed thereunder by subsequent individual agreements. These territories are hereinafter referred to as trust territories.

Article 76

The basic objectives of the trusteeship system, in accordance with the Purposes of the United Nations laid down in Article 1 of the present Charter, shall be:

(a) to further international peace and security;

(b) to promote the political, economic, social, and educational advancement of the inhabitants of the trust territories, and their progressive development towards self-government or independence as may be appropriate to the particular circumstances of each territory and its peoples and the freely expressed wishes of the peoples concerned, and as may be provided by the terms of each trusteeship agreement;

(c) to encourage respect for human rights and for fundamental freedoms for all without distinction as to race, sex, language, or religion, and to encourage recognition of the interdependence of the peoples of the world; and

(d) to ensure equal treatment in social, economic, and commercial matters for all Members of the United Nations and their nationals, and also equal treatment for the latter in the administration of justice, without prejudice to the attainment of the foregoing objectives and subject to the provisions of Article 80.

Article 77

1. The trusteeship system shall apply to such territories in the following categories as may be placed thereunder by means of trusteeship agreements:

(a) territories now held under mandate;

(b) territories which may be detached from enemy states as a result of the Second World War; and

(c) territories voluntarily placed under the system by states responsible for their administration.

2. It will be a matter for subsequent agreement as to which territories in the foregoing categories will be brought under the trusteeship system and upon what terms.

Article 78

The trusteeship system shall not apply to territories which have become Members of the United Nations, relationship among which shall be based on respect for the principle of sovereign equality.

Article 79

The terms of trusteeship for each territory to be placed under the trusteeship system, including any alteration or amendment, shall be agreed upon by the states directly concerned, including the mandatory power in the case of territories held under mandate by a Member of the United Nations, and shall be approved as provided for in Articles 83 and 85.

Article 80

1. Except as may be agreed upon in individual trusteeship agreements, made under Articles 77, 79, and 81, placing each territory under the trusteeship system, and until such agreements have been concluded, nothing in this Chapter shall be construed in or of itself to alter in any manner the rights whatsoever of any states

or any peoples or the terms of existing international instruments to which Members of the United Nations may respectively be parties.

2. Paragraph 1 of this Article shall not be interpreted as giving grounds for delay or postponement of the negotiation and conclusion of agreements for placing mandated and other territories under the trusteeship system as provided for in Article 77.

Article 81

The trusteeship agreement shall in each case include the terms under which the trust territory will be administered and designate the authority which will exercise the administration of the trust territory. Such authority, hereinafter called the administering authority, may be one or more states or the Organization itself.

Article 82

There may be designated, in any trusteeship agreement, a strategic area or areas which may include part or all of the trust territory to which the agreement applies, without prejudice to any special agreement or agreements made under Article 43.

Article 83

1. All functions of the United Nations relating to strategic areas, including the approval of the terms of the trusteeship agreements and of their alteration or amendment, shall be exercised by the Security Council.

2. The basic objectives set forth in Article 76 shall be applicable to the people of each strategic area.

3. The Security Council shall, subject to the provisions of the trusteeship agreements and without prejudice to security considerations, avail itself of the assistance of the Trusteeship Council to perform those functions of the United Nations under the trusteeship system relating to political, economic, social, and educational matters in the strategic areas.

Article 84

It shall be the duty of the administering authority to ensure that the trust territory shall play its part in the maintenance of international peace and security. To this end the administering authority may make use of volunteer forces, facilities, and assistance from the trust territory in carrying out the obligations towards the Security Council undertaken in this regard by the administering authority, as well as for local defense and the maintenance of law and order within the trust territory.

Article 85

1. The functions of the United Nations with regard to trusteeship agreements for all areas not designated as strategic, including the approval of the terms of the trusteeship agreements and of their alteration or amendment, shall be exercised by the General Assembly.

2. The Trusteeship Council, operating under the authority of the General Assembly, shall assist the General Assembly in carrying out these functions.

CHAPTER XIII

THE TRUSTEESHIP COUNCIL
COMPOSITION

Article 86

1. The Trusteeship Council shall consist of the following Members of the United Nations:

(a) those Members administering trust territories;

(b) such of those Members mentioned by name in Article 23 as are not administering trust territories; and

(c) as many other Members elected for three-year terms by the General Assembly as may be necessary to ensure that the total number of members of the Trusteeship Council is equally divided between those Members of the United Nations which administer trust territories and those which do not.

2. Each member of the Trusteeship Council shall designate one specially qualified person to represent it therein.

FUNCTIONS AND POWERS

Article 87

The General Assembly and, under its authority, the Trusteeship Council, in carrying out their functions, may:

(a) consider reports submitted by the administering authority;

(b) accept petitions and examine them in consultation with the administering authority;

(c) provide for periodic visits to the respective trust territories at times agreed upon with the administering authority; and

(d) take these and other actions in conformity with the terms of the trusteeship agreements.

Article 88

The Trusteeship Council shall formulate a questionnaire on the political, economic, social, and educational advancement of the inhabitants of each trust territory, and the administering authority for each trust territory within the competence of the General Assembly shall make an annual report to the General Assembly upon the basis of such questionnaire.

VOTING

Article 89

1. Each member of the Trusteeship Council shall have one vote.
2. Decisions of the Trusteeship Council shall be made by a majority of the members present and voting.

PROCEDURE

Article 90

1. The Trusteeship Council shall adopt its own rules of procedure, including the method of selecting its President.
2. The Trusteeship Council shall meet as required in accordance with its rules, which shall include provision for the convening of meetings on the request of a majority of its members.

Article 91

The Trusteeship Council shall, when appropriate, avail itself of the assistance of the Economic and Social Council and of the specialized agencies in regard to matters with which they are respectively concerned.

CHAPTER XIV

THE INTERNATIONAL COURT OF JUSTICE

Article 92

The International Court of Justice shall be the principal judicial organ of the United Nations. It shall function in accordance with the annexed Statute, which is based upon the Statute of the Permanent Court of International Justice and forms an integral part of the present Charter.

Article 93

1. All Members of the United Nations are *ipso facto* parties to the Statute of the International Court of Justice.

2. A state which is not a Member of the United Nations may become a party to the Statute of the International Court of Justice on conditions to be determined in each case by the General Assembly upon the recommendation of the Security Council.

Article 94

1. Each Member of the United Nations undertakes to comply with the decision of the International Court of Justice in any case to which it is a party.

2. If any party to a case fails to perform the obligations incumbent upon it under a judgment rendered by the Court, the other party may have recourse to the Security Council, which may, if it deems necessary, make recommendations or decide upon measures to be taken to give effect to the judgment.

Article 95

Nothing in the present Charter shall prevent Members of the United Nations from entrusting the solution of their differences to other tribunals by virtue of agreements already in existence or which may be concluded in the future.

Article 96

1. The General Assembly or the Security Council may request the International Court of Justice to give an advisory opinion on any legal question.

2. Other organs of the United Nations and specialized agencies, which may at any time be so authorized by the General Assembly, may also request advisory opinions of the Court on legal questions arising within the scope of their activities.

CHAPTER XV

THE SECRETARIAT

Article 97

The Secretariat shall comprise a Secretary-General and such staff as the Organization may require. The Secretary-General shall be appointed by the General Assembly upon the recommendation of the Security Council. He shall be the chief administrative officer of the Organization.

Article 98

The Secretary-General shall act in that capacity in all meetings of the General Assembly, of the Security Council, of the Economic and Social Council, and of the Trusteeship Council, and shall perform such other functions as are entrusted to him by these organs. The Secretary-General shall make an annual report to the General Assembly on the work of the Organization.

Article 99

The Secretary-General may bring to the attention of the Security Council any matter which in his opinion may threaten the maintenance of international peace and security.

Article 100

1. In the performance of their duties the Secretary-General and the staff shall not seek or receive instructions from any government or from any other authority external to the Organization. They shall refrain from any action which might reflect on their position as international officials responsible only to the Organization.

2. Each Member of the United Nations undertakes to respect the exclusively international character of the responsibilities of the

Secretary-General and the staff and not to seek to influence them in the discharge of their responsibilities.

Article 101

1. The staff shall be appointed by the Secretary-General under regulations established by the General Assembly.

2. Appropriate staffs shall be permanently assigned to the Economic and Social Council, the Trusteeship Council, and, as required, to other organs of the United Nations. These staffs shall form a part of the Secretariat.

3. The paramount consideration in the employment of the staff and in the determination of the conditions of service shall be the necessity of securing the highest standards of efficiency, competence, and integrity. Due regard shall be paid to the importance of recruiting the staff on as wide a geographical basis as possible.

CHAPTER XVI

MISCELLANEOUS PROVISIONS

Article 102

1. Every treaty and every international agreement entered into by any Member of the United Nations after the present Charter comes into force shall as soon as possible be registered with the Secretariat and published by it.

2. No party to any such treaty or international agreement which has not been registered in accordance with the provisions of paragraph 1 of this Article may invoke that treaty or agreement before any organ of the United Nations.

Article 103

In the event of a conflict between the obligations of the Members of the United Nations under the present Charter and their obligations under any other international agreement, their obligations under the present Charter shall prevail.

Article 104

The Organization shall enjoy in the territory of each of its Members such legal capacity as may be necessary for the exercise of its functions and the fulfillment of its purposes.

Article 105

1. The Organization shall enjoy in the territory of each of its Members such privileges and immunities as are necessary for the fulfillment of its purposes.

2. Representatives of the Members of the United Nations and officials of the Organization shall similarly enjoy such privileges and immunities as are necessary for the independent exercise of their functions in connection with the Organization.

3. The General Assembly may make recommendations with a view to determining the details of the application of paragraphs 1 and 2 of this Article or may propose conventions to the Members of the United Nations for this purpose.

CHAPTER XVII

TRANSITIONAL SECURITY ARRANGEMENTS

Article 106

Pending the coming into force of such special agreements referred to in Article 43 as in the opinion of the Security Council enable it to begin the exercise of its responsibilities under Article 42, the parties to the Four-Nation Declaration, signed at Moscow, October 30, 1943, and France, shall, in accordance with the provisions of paragraph 5 of that Declaration, consult with one another and as occasion requires with other Members of the United Nations with a view to such joint action on behalf of the Organization as may be necessary for the purpose of maintaining international peace and security.

Article 107

Nothing in the present Charter shall invalidate or preclude action, in relation to any state which during the Second World War has been an enemy of any signatory to the present Charter, taken or authorized as a result of that war by the Governments having responsibility for such action.

CHAPTER XVIII

AMENDMENTS

Article 108

Amendments to the present Charter shall come into force for all Members of the United Nations when they have been adopted by a vote of two thirds of the members of the General Assembly and ratified in accordance with their respective constitutional processes by two thirds of the Members of the United Nations, including all the permanent members of the Security Council.

Article 109

1. A General Conference of the Members of the United Nations for the purpose of reviewing the present Charter may be held at a date and place to be fixed by a two-thirds vote of the members of the General Assembly and by a vote of any seven members of the Security Council. Each Member of the United Nations shall have one vote in the conference.

2. Any alteration of the present Charter recommended by a two-thirds vote of the conference shall take effect when ratified in

accordance with their respective constitutional processes by two thirds of the Members of the United Nations including all the permanent members of the Security Council.

3. If such a conference has not been held before the tenth annual session of the General Assembly following the coming into force of the present Charter, the proposal to call such a conference shall be placed on the agenda of that session of the General Assembly, and the conference shall be held if so decided by a majority vote of the members of the General Assembly and by a vote of any seven members of the Security Council.

CHAPTER XIX

RATIFICATION AND SIGNATURE

Article 110

1. The present Charter shall be ratified by the signatory states in accordance with their respective constitutional processes.

2. The ratifications shall be deposited with the Government of the United States of America, which shall notify all the signatory states of each deposit as well as the Secretary-General of the Organization when he has been appointed.

3. The present Charter shall come into force upon the deposit of ratifications by the Republic of China, France, the Union of Soviet Socialist Republics, the United Kingdom of Great Britain and Northern Ireland, and the United States of America, and by a majority of the other signatory states. A protocol of the ratifications deposited shall thereupon be drawn up by the Government of the United States of America which shall communicate copies thereof to all the signatory states.

4. The states signatory to the present Charter which ratify it after it has come into force will become original Members of the United Nations on the date of the deposit of their respective ratifications.

Article 111

The present Charter of which the Chinese, French, Russian, English, and Spanish texts are equally authentic, shall remain deposited in the archives of the Government of the United States of America. Duly certified copies thereof shall be transmitted by that Government to the Governments of the other signatory states.

IN FAITH WHEREOF the representatives of the Governments of the United Nations have signed the present Charter.

DONE at the city of San Francisco the twenty-sixth day of June, one thousand nine hundred and forty-five.

STATUTE OF THE INTERNATIONAL COURT OF JUSTICE

(Every nation that ratifies the Charter of the United Nations, automatically accepts this Statute, too.)

Article 1

THE INTERNATIONAL COURT OF JUSTICE established by the Charter of the United Nations as the principal judicial organ of the United Nations shall be constituted and shall function in accordance with the provisions of the present Statute.

CHAPTER I

ORGANIZATION OF THE COURT

Article 2

The Court shall be composed of a body of independent judges, elected regardless of their nationality from among persons of high moral character, who possess the qualifications required in their respective countries for appointment to the highest judicial offices, or are juris-consults of recognized competence in international law.

Article 3

1. The Court shall consist of fifteen members, no two of whom may be nationals of the same state.

2. A person who for the purposes of membership in the Court could be regarded as a national of more than one state shall be deemed to be a national of the one in which he ordinarily exercises civil and political rights.

Article 4

1. The members of the Court shall be elected by the General Assembly and by the Security Council from a list of persons nominated by the national groups in the Permanent Court of Arbitration, in accordance with the following provisions.

2. In the case of Members of the United Nations not represented in the Permanent Court of Arbitration, candidates shall be nominated by national groups appointed for this purpose by their governments under the same conditions as those prescribed for members of the Permanent Court of Arbitration by Article 44 of the Convention of The Hague of 1907 for the pacific settlement of international disputes.

3. The conditions under which a state which is a party to the present Statute but is not a Member of the United Nations may participate in electing the members of the Court shall, in the absence of a special agreement, be laid down by the General Assembly upon recommendation of the Security Council.

Article 5

1. At least three months before the date of the election, the Secretary-General of the United Nations shall address a written request

to the members of the Permanent Court of Arbitration belonging to the states which are parties to the present Statute, and to the members of the national groups appointed under Article 4, paragraph 2, inviting them to undertake, within a given time, by national groups, the nomination of persons in a position to accept the duties of a member of the Court.

2. No group may nominate more than four persons, not more than two of whom shall be of their own nationality. In no case may the number of candidates nominated by a group be more than double the number of seats to be filled.

Article 6

Before making these nominations, each national group is recommended to consult its highest court of justice, its legal faculties and schools of law, and its national academies and national sections of international academies devoted to the study of law.

Article 7

1. The Secretary-General shall prepare a list in alphabetical order of all the persons thus nominated. Save as provided in Article 12, paragraph 2, these shall be the only persons eligible.

2. The Secretary-General shall submit this list to the General Assembly and to the Security Council.

Article 8

The General Assembly and the Security Council shall proceed independently of one another to elect the members of the Court.

Article 9

At every election, the electors shall bear in mind not only that the persons to be elected should individually possess the qualifications required, but also that in the body as a whole the representation of the main forms of civilization and of the principal legal systems of the world should be assured.

Article 10

1. Those candidates who obtain an absolute majority of votes in the General Assembly and in the Security Council shall be considered as elected.

2. Any vote of the Security Council, whether for the election of judges or for the appointment of members of the conference envisaged in Article 12, shall be taken without any distinction between permanent and non-permanent members of the Security Council.

3. In the event of more than one national of the same state obtaining an absolute majority of the votes both of the General Assembly and of the Security Council, the eldest of these only shall be considered as elected.

Article 11

If, after the first meeting held for the purpose of the election, one or more seats remain to be filled, a second and, if necessary, a third meeting shall take place.

Article 12

1. If, after the third meeting, one or more seats still remain unfilled, a joint conference consisting of six members, three appointed by the General Assembly and three by the Security Council, may be formed at any time at the request of either the General Assembly or the Security Council, for the purpose of choosing by the vote of an absolute majority one name for each seat still vacant, to submit to the General Assembly and the Security Council for their respective acceptance.

2. If the joint conference is unanimously agreed upon any person who fulfils the required conditions, he may be included in its list,

even though he was not included in the list of nominations referred to in Article 7.

3. If the joint conference is satisfied that it will not be successful in procuring an election, those members of the Court who have already been elected shall, within a period to be fixed by the Security Council, proceed to fill the vacant seats by selection from among those candidates who have obtained votes either in the General Assembly or in the Security Council.

4. In the event of an equality of votes among the judges, the eldest judge shall have a casting vote.

Article 13

1. The members of the Court shall be elected for nine years and may be re-elected; provided, however, that of the judges elected at the first election, the terms of five judges shall expire at the end of three years and the terms of five more judges shall expire at the end of six years.

2. The judges whose terms are to expire at the end of the above-mentioned initial period of three and six years shall be chosen by lot to be drawn by the Secretary-General immediately after the first election has been completed.

3. The members of the Court shall continue to discharge their duties until their places have been filled. Though replaced, they shall finish any cases which they may have begun.

4. In the case of the resignation of a member of the Court, the resignation shall be addressed to the President of the Court for transmission to the Secretary-General. This last notification makes the place vacant.

Article 14

Vacancies shall be filled by the same method as that laid down for the first election, subject to the following provision: the Secretary-General shall, within one month of the occurrence of the vacancy, proceed to issue the invitations provided for in Article 5, and the date of the election shall be fixed by the Security Council.

Article 15

A member of the Court elected to replace a member whose term of office has not expired shall hold office for the remainder of his predecessor's term.

Article 16

1. No member of the Court may exercise any political or administrative function, or engage in any other occupation of a professional nature.

2. Any doubt on this point shall be settled by the decision of the Court.

Article 17

1. No member of the Court may act as agent, counsel, or advocate in any case.

2. No member may participate in the decision of any case in which he has previously taken part as agent, counsel, or advocate for one of the parties, or as a member of a national or international court, or of a commission of enquiry, or in any other capacity.

3. Any doubt on this point shall be settled by the decision of the Court.

Article 18

1. No member of the Court can be dismissed unless, in the unanimous opinion of the other members, he has ceased to fulfil the required conditions.

2. Formal notification thereof shall be made to the Secretary-General by the Registrar.

3. This notification makes the place vacant.

Article 19

The members of the Court, when engaged on the business of the Court, shall enjoy diplomatic privileges and immunities.

Article 20

Every member of the Court shall, before taking up his duties, make a solemn declaration in open court that he will exercise his powers impartially and conscientiously.

Article 21

1. The Court shall elect its President and Vice-President for three years; they may be re-elected.

2. The Court shall appoint its Registrar and may provide for the appointment of such other officers as may be necessary.

Article 22

1. The seat of the Court shall be established at The Hague. This, however, shall not prevent the Court from sitting and exercising its functions elsewhere whenever the Court considers it desirable.

2. The President and the Registrar shall reside at the seat of the Court.

Article 23

1. The Court shall remain permanently in session, except during the judicial vacations, the dates and duration of which shall be fixed by the Court.

2. Members of the Court are entitled to periodic leave, the dates and duration of which shall be fixed by the Court, having in mind the distance between The Hague and the home of each judge.

3. Members of the Court shall be bound, unless they are on leave or prevented from attending by illness or other serious reasons duly explained to the President, to hold themselves permanently at the disposal of the Court.

Article 24

1. If, for some special reason, a member of the Court considers that he should not take part in the decision of a particular case, he shall so inform the President.

2. If the President considers that for some special reason one of the members of the Court should not sit in a particular case, he shall give him notice accordingly.

3. If in any such case the member of the Court and the President disagree, the matter shall be settled by the decision of the Court.

Article 25

1. The full Court shall sit except when it is expressly provided otherwise in the present Statute.

2. Subject to the condition that the number of judges available to constitute the Court is not thereby reduced below eleven, the Rules of the Court may provide for allowing one or more judges, according to circumstances and in rotation, to be dispensed from sitting.

3. A quorum of nine judges shall suffice to constitute the Court.

Article 26

1. The Court may from time to time form one or more chambers, composed of three or more judges as the Court may determine, for dealing with particular categories of cases; for example, labor cases and cases relating to transit and communications.

2. The Court may at any time form a chamber for dealing with a particular case. The number of judges to constitute such a cham-

ber shall be determined by the Court with the approval of the parties.

3. Cases shall be heard and determined by the chambers provided for in this Article if the parties so request.

Article 27

A judgment given by any of the chambers provided for in Articles 26 and 29 shall be considered as rendered by the Court.

Article 28

The chambers provided for in Articles 26 and 29 may, with the consent of the parties, sit and exercise their functions elsewhere than at The Hague.

Article 29

With a view to the speedy despatch of business, the Court shall form annually a chamber composed of five judges which, at the request of the parties, may hear and determine cases by summary procedure. In addition, two judges shall be selected for the purpose of replacing judges who find it impossible to sit.

Article 30

1. The Court shall frame rules for carrying out its functions. In particular, it shall lay down rules of procedure.

2. The rules of the Court may provide for assessors to sit with the Court or with any of its chambers, without the right to vote.

Article 31

1. Judges of the nationality of each of the parties shall retain their right to sit in the case before the Court.

2. If the Court includes upon the Bench a judge of the nationality of one of the parties, any other party may choose a person to sit as

judge. Such person shall be chosen preferably from among those persons who have been nominated as candidates as provided in Articles 4 and 5.

3. If the Court includes upon the Bench no judge of the nationality of the parties, each of these parties may proceed to choose a judge as provided in paragraph 2 of this Article.

4. The provisions of this Article shall apply to the case of Articles 26 and 29. In such cases, the President shall request one or, if necessary, two of the members of the court forming the chamber to give place to the members of the Court of the nationality of the parties concerned, and, failing such, or if they are unable to be present, to the judges specially chosen by the parties.

5. Should there be several parties in the same interest, they shall, for the purpose of the preceding provisions, be reckoned as one party only. Any doubt upon this point shall be settled by the decision of the Court.

6. Judges chosen as laid down in paragraphs 2, 3, and 4 of this Article shall fulfil the conditions required by Articles 2, 17 (paragraph 2), 20, and 24 of the present Statute. They shall take part in the decision on terms of complete equality with their colleagues.

Article 32

1. Each member of the Court shall receive an annual salary.

2. The President shall receive a special annual allowance.

3. The Vice-President shall receive a special allowance for every day on which he acts as President.

4. The judges chosen under Article 31, other than members of the Court, shall receive compensation for each day on which they exercise their functions.

5. These salaries, allowances, and compensation shall be fixed by the General Assembly. They may not be decreased during the term of office.

6. The salary of the Registrar shall be fixed by the General Assembly on the proposal of the Court.

7. Regulations made by the General Assembly shall fix the conditions under which retirement pensions may be given to members of the Court and to the Registrar, and the conditions under which members of the Court and the Registrar shall have their traveling expenses refunded.

8. The above salaries, allowances, and compensation shall be free of all taxation.

Article 33

The expenses of the Court shall be borne by the United Nations in such a manner as shall be decided by the General Assembly.

CHAPTER II

COMPETENCE OF THE COURT

Article 34

1. Only states may be parties in cases before the Court.

2. The Court, subject to and in conformity with its Rules, may request of public international organizations information relevant to cases before it, and shall receive such information presented by such organizations on their own initiative.

3. Whenever the construction of the constituent instrument of a public international organization or of an international convention adopted thereunder is in question in a case before the Court, the Registrar shall so notify the public international organization concerned and shall communicate to it copies of all the written proceedings.

Article 35

1. The Court shall be open to the states parties to the present Statute.

2. The conditions under which the Court shall be open to other

states shall, subject to the special provisions contained in treaties in force, be laid down by the Security Council, but in no case shall such conditions place the parties in a position of inequality before the Court.

3. When a state which is not a Member of the United Nations is a party to a case, the Court shall fix the amount which that party is to contribute towards the expenses of the Court. This provision shall not apply if such state is bearing a share of the expenses of the Court.

Article 36

1. The jurisdiction of the Court comprises all cases which the parties refer to it and all matters specially provided for in the Charter of the United Nations or in treaties and conventions in force.

2. The states parties to the present Statute may at any time declare that they recognize as compulsory *ipso facto* and without special agreement, in relation to any other state accepting the same obligation, the jurisdiction of the Court in all legal disputes concerning:

(a) the interpretation of a treaty;

(b) any question of international law;

(c) the existence of any fact which, if established, would constitute a breach of an international obligation;

(d) the nature or extent of the reparation to be made for the breach of an international obligation.

3. The declarations referred to above may be made unconditionally or on condition of reciprocity on the part of several or certain states, or for a certain time.

4. Such declarations shall be deposited with the Secretary-General of the United Nations, who shall transmit copies thereof to the parties to the Statute and to the Registrar of the Court.

5. Declarations made under Article 36 of the Statute of the Permanent Court of International Justice and which are still in force shall be deemed, as between the parties to the present Statute, to be acceptances of the compulsory jurisdiction of the International

Court of Justice for the period which they still have to run and in accordance with their terms.

6. In the event of a dispute as to whether the Court has jurisdiction, the matter shall be settled by the decision of the Court.

Article 37

Whenever a treaty or convention in force provides for reference of a matter to a tribunal to have been instituted by the League of Nations, or to the Permanent Court of International Justice, the matter shall, as between the parties to the present Statute, be referred to the International Court of Justice.

Article 38

1. The Court, whose function is to decide in accordance with international law such disputes as are submitted to it, shall apply:

(a) international conventions, whether general or particular, establishing rules expressly recognized by the contesting states;

(b) international custom, as evidence of a general practice accepted as law;

(c) the general principles of law recognized by civilized nations;

(d) subject to the provisions of Article 59, judicial decisions and the teachings of the most highly qualified publicists of the various nations, as subsidiary means for the determination of rules of law.

2. This provision shall not prejudice the power of the Court to decide a case *ex aequo et bono*, if the parties agree thereto.

CHAPTER III

PROCEDURE

Article 39

1. The official languages of the Court shall be French and English. If the parties agree that the case shall be conducted in French,

the judgment shall be delivered in French. If the parties agree that the case shall be conducted in English, the judgment shall be delivered in English.

2. In the absence of an agreement as to which language shall be employed, each party may, in the pleadings, use the language which it prefers; the decision of the Court shall be given in French and English. In this case the Court shall at the same time determine which of the two texts shall be considered as authoritative.

3. The Court shall, at the request of any party, authorize a language other than French or English to be used by that party.

Article 40

1. Cases are brought before the Court, as the case may be, either by the notification of the special agreement or by a written application addressed to the Registrar. In either case the subject of the dispute and the parties shall be indicated.

2. The Registrar shall forthwith communicate the application to all concerned.

3. He shall also notify the Members of the United Nations through the Secretary-General, and also any other states entitled to appear before the Court.

Article 41

1. The Court shall have the power to indicate, if it considers that circumstances so require, any provisional measures which ought to be taken to preserve the respective rights of either party.

2. Pending the final decision, notice of the measures suggested shall forthwith be given to the parties and to the Security Council.

Article 42

1. The parties shall be represented by agents.

2. They may have the assistance of counsel or advocates before the Court.

3. The agents, counsel, and advocates of parties before the Court shall enjoy the privileges and immunities necessary to the independent exercise of their duties.

Article 43

1. The procedure shall consist of two parts: written and oral.

2. The written proceedings shall consist of the communication to the Court and to the parties of memorials, counter-memorials and, if necessary, replies; also all papers and documents in support.

3. These communications shall be made through the Registrar, in the order and within the time fixed by the Court.

4. A certified copy of every document produced by one party shall be communicated to the other party.

5. The oral proceedings shall consist of the hearing by the Court of witnesses, experts, agents, counsel, and advocates.

Article 44

1. For the service of all notices upon persons other than the agents, counsel, and advocates, the Court shall apply direct to the government of the state upon whose territory the notice has to be served.

2. The same provision shall apply whenever steps are to be taken to procure evidence on the spot.

Article 45

The hearing shall be under the control of the President or, if he is unable to preside, of the Vice-President; if neither is able to preside, the senior judge present shall preside.

Article 46

The hearing in Court shall be public, unless the Court shall decide otherwise, or unless the parties demand that the public be not admitted.

Article 47

1. Minutes shall be made at each hearing and signed by the Registrar and the President.

2. These minutes alone shall be authentic.

Article 48

The Court shall make orders for the conduct of the case, shall decide the form and time in which each party must conclude its arguments, and make all arrangements connected with the taking of evidence.

Article 49

The Court may, even before the hearing begins, call upon the agents to produce any document or to supply any explanations. Formal note shall be taken of any refusal.

Article 50

The Court may, at any time, entrust any individual, body, bureau, commission, or other organization that it may select, with the task of carrying out an enquiry or giving an expert opinion.

Article 51

During the hearing any relevant questions are to be put to the witnesses and experts under the conditions laid down by the Court in the rules of procedure referred to in Article 30.

Article 52

After the Court has received the proofs and evidence within the time specified for the purpose, it may refuse to accept any further oral or written evidence that one party may desire to present unless the other side consents.

Article 53

1. Whenever one of the parties does not appear before the Court, or fails to defend its case, the other party may call upon the Court to decide in favor of its claim.

2. The Court must, before doing so, satisfy itself, not only that it has jurisdiction in accordance with Articles 36 and 37, but also that the claim is well founded in fact and law.

Article 54

1. When, subject to the control of the Court, the agents, counsel, and advocates have completed their presentation of the case, the President shall declare the hearing closed.

2. The Court shall withdraw to consider the judgment.

3. The deliberations of the Court shall take place in private and remain secret.

Article 55

1. All questions shall be decided by a majority of the judges present.

2. In the event of an equality of votes, the President or the judge who acts in his place shall have a casting vote.

Article 56

1. The judgment shall state the reasons on which it is based.

2. It shall contain the names of the judges who have taken part in the decision.

Article 57

If the judgment does not represent in whole or in part the unanimous opinion of the judges, any judge shall be entitled to deliver a separate opinion.

Article 58

The judgment shall be signed by the President and by the Registrar. It shall be read in open court, due notice having been given to the agents.

Article 59

The decision of the Court has no binding force except between the parties and in respect of that particular case.

Article 60

The judgment is final and without appeal. In the event of dispute as to the meaning or scope of the judgment, the Court shall construe it upon the request of any party.

Article 61

1. An application for revision of a judgment may be made only when it is based upon the discovery of some fact of such a nature as to be a decisive factor, which fact was, when the judgment was given, unknown to the Court and also to the party claiming revision, always provided that such ignorance was not due to negligence.

2. The proceedings for revision shall be opened by a judgment of the Court expressly recording the existence of the new fact, recognizing that it has such a character as to lay the case open to revision, and declaring the application admissible on this ground.

3. The Court may require previous compliance with the terms of the judgment before it admits proceedings in revision.

4. The application for revision must be made at latest within six months of the discovery of the new fact.

5. No application for revision may be made after the lapse of ten years from the date of the judgment.

Article 62

1. Should a state consider that it has an interest of a legal nature which may be affected by the decision in the case, it may submit a request to the Court to be permitted to intervene.

2. It shall be for the Court to decide upon this request.

Article 63

1. Whenever the construction of a convention to which states other than those concerned in the case are parties is in question, the Registrar shall notify all such states forthwith.

2. Every state so notified has the right to intervene in the proceedings; but if it uses this right, the construction given by the judgment will be equally binding upon it.

Article 64

Unless otherwise decided by the Court, each party shall bear its own costs.

CHAPTER IV

ADVISORY OPINIONS

Article 65

1. The Court may give an advisory opinion on any legal question at the request of whatever body may be authorized by or in accordance with the Charter of the United Nations to make such a request.

2. Questions upon which the advisory opinion of the Court is asked shall be laid before the Court by means of a written request

containing an exact statement of the question upon which an opinion is required, and accompanied by all documents likely to throw light upon the question.

Article 66

1. The Registrar shall forthwith give notice of the request for an advisory opinion to all states entitled to appear before the Court.

2. The Registrar shall also, by means of a special and direct communication, notify any state entitled to appear before the Court or international organization considered by the Court, or, should it not be sitting, by the President, as likely to be able to furnish information on the question, that the Court will be prepared to receive, within a time limit to be fixed by the President, written statements, or to hear, at a public sitting to be held for the purpose, oral statements relating to the question.

3. Should any such state entitled to appear before the Court have failed to receive the special communication referred to in paragraph 2 of this Article, such state may express a desire to submit a written statement or to be heard; and the Court will decide.

4. States and organizations having presented written or oral statements or both shall be permitted to comment on the statements made by other states or organizations in the form, to the extent, and within the time limits which the Court, or, should it not be sitting, the President, shall decide in each particular case. Accordingly, the Registrar shall in due time communicate any such written statements to states and organizations having submitted similar statements.

Article 67

The Court shall deliver its advisory opinions in open court, notice having been given to the Secretary-General and to the representatives of Members of the United Nations, of other states and of international organizations immediately concerned.

Article 68

In the exercise of its advisory functions the Court shall further be guided by the provisions of the present Statute which apply in contentious cases to the extent to which it recognizes them to be applicable.

CHAPTER V

AMENDMENT

Article 69

Amendments to the present Statute shall be effected by the same procedure as is provided by the Charter of the United Nations for amendments to that Charter, subject however to any provisions which the General Assembly upon recommendation of the Security Council may adopt concerning the participation of states which are parties to the present Statute but are not Members of the United Nations.

Article 70

The Court shall have power to propose such amendments to the present Statute as it may deem necessary, through written communications to the Secretary-General, for consideration in conformity with the provisions of Article 69.

INDEX

ABOUT THE AUTHOR

Tom Galt, author of well-known works of history and biography, was born in Michigan and brought up in St. Louis. He was graduated from Harvard and for eight years was a teacher and librarian at the Fieldston School in New York.

In addition to his writing, he has lectured widely on economics and international relations. Three summers spent in Mexico resulted in the writing of pamphlets for the Pan American Union, and his first book for children, *Volcano*.

Mr. Galt lives in New York and devotes all his working time to writing. Between books he and his wife are usually on the road or in the air. He delights in the art museums, the music, and the theaters of each country he visits, and as an accomplished linguist is able to enjoy these pleasures to the full. His *How the United Nations Works* and *Peter Zenger: Fighter for Freedom* have been published in nineteen languages, and when Mr. Galt and his wife took an extended trip to Japan, Hong Kong, India, and around the world, they visited the offices where the translations were made.

Mr. Galt is now at work on a scholarly biography of Molière.

DATE DUE